The Dance Of Imperfection

Living In Perfect Harmony With Life

Alex P. Keats

Right Now
Publishing

Right Now Publishing
ISBN - 13: 978-0615949130
ISBN - 10: 0615949134

First Printing, 2012
Printed in the United States of America

Other Books by Alex P. Keats:

Born To Be Happy
How to Uncover Your Natural State of Happiness

If we really are born to be happy, then why is it so elusive to so many of us? Is happiness really dependent upon the circumstances in our lives - or is there more to it than that? How do our beliefs and our past affect our ability to be truly happy? "*Born To Be Happy - How to Uncover Your Natural State of Happiness*" by Alex P. Keats, explores these questions in depth and will help you discover how to live in harmony with the happiness that's already your natural state.

Tapping into both ancient wisdom and your inner wisdom that already knows what's true, you'll understand why so many methods and strategies for happiness are short-lived and fleeting. As a result, you'll be armed with the knowledge that opens the floodgates to your natural state of happiness ... and your life will never be the same.

When Wisdom Blooms
Awaken The Sage Within

When we're born, we didn't come with an operating manual showing us how to live from our natural state of wisdom. All the parts were in the box, but the directions were left out. And since most around us still haven't cracked the code, it's no wonder why we experience so many challenges in life.

And yet if wisdom really is fully present and available within each one of us, why does it seem so difficult to access and live from? Wisdom is the power to see what is always and already right and true. It's that aspect of our self that innately possesses the ability to discern truth from falsehood.

If wisdom is a flower that only blossoms under the proper conditions, we are wise to know what those conditions are. Conversely, we are wise to notice what suppresses our innate wisdom so that it's opposite quality, ignorance, doesn't blossom. Wouldn't the quality of our lives then, ultimately be dependent upon which half blooms? What might happen if we put aside everything we've accumulated up to this point, and suspend all that we think we know for a time, for the very real possibility of experiencing a different reality, right now? Well, let’s find out.

Dedication

This book is dedicated to Susan, Molly and Puff. None of this would be possible if it weren't for you.

"Re-examine all you have been told in school, in church or any book, and dismiss whatever insults your soul, and your very flesh shall become a great poem, and have the richest fluency, not only in its words, but in the silent lines of its lips and face, and between the lashes of your eyes, and in every motion and joint of your body."

~ **Walt Whitman**

Contents

Introduction

From my late teens to my early thirties, I was an active alcoholic. Somehow I didn't connect my depression and low self-esteem with my weekend use of alcohol. Not only did it bring a lot of pain and suffering for me, but for those who loved me as well. I traded peace and happiness for short-term highs that led to fifteen-year lows, sometimes devastating lows.

When I finally realized that alcoholism is a disease with signs and symptoms - possessing a morbid process - and that it takes over your will and ability to choose, something inside radically shifted. Where for so many years I experienced deep shame, guilt and remorse for behaviors that sometimes shocked me, it all dissolved in a deep realization that I wasn't consciously doing any of it.

I was powerless over the disease that held me in its grips. I wasn't to blame for my addiction, but I was responsible to get the support I needed. Seeing the nature of the situation, it made perfect sense why I did what I did; and it explained why I felt as I did. It made perfect sense that my life never got on track. How could it? I was addicted to alcohol and its consequences - and I wasn't pulling my own strings. Finally seeing that I wasn't in the driver's seat, and that I wasn't intentionally destroying my life, something of a higher order moved in. Permanently.

It was no coincidence that when the truth of the situation was seen, real healing began - the kind that effected long term change. Low self-esteem was on its way out, and in its place, a complete acceptance of who I was, as I was, came flooding in. Some people would think alcoholism is an imperfection. I don't see it that way. Are diabetes, cancer and heart disease imperfections? How about stuttering, dyslexia, autism, depression and chronic anxiety? Are they imperfections, too?

Like alcoholism, they're just conditions we call "disease" or "disorder. Some would say that it's a matter of semantics, and that it's all the same, just worded differently. If that's the case, then why do we feel insecure and self-conscious when we perceive and therefore, label aspects of ourselves "imperfect" or "inadequate?" How else can we feel *but* insecure?

In other words, if we didn't perceive and label aspects of ourselves as imperfect or flawed, would we still feel less than and unworthy? No, we wouldn't. What about those aspects of yourself you don't really like? Are they really and truly imperfections? When we *see* what's true, when we *realize* that any aspect of ourselves is simply that, just an aspect, as it is, we liberate ourselves from our mind that insists we can be different than we presently are.

We liberate ourselves from feeling unworthy and not up to par, too. We overlook that while things are often different than they *were*, and often different than they *will be*, they are never different than they *are* in this present moment. Can we live outside the present moment?

When we see that as long as we continue to judge and condemn aspects of ourselves (and others) - as they are - we hold in place what we don't want. Our resistance and judgments are wasted energy that gives life to what we'd rather not experience. Since we can never escape our interpretations, misperception also gives life to what we don't want. It's felt in the body, indicating that we aren't in harmony with life and the law of our experience. What we perceive, we receive. Whatever we resist and condemn, persists and binds us. Whatever we face and embrace dissolves and lets go of us. Thus, our perception either enslaves or frees.

Truth frees while illusion enslaves. You have this capability of self-examination. Look beyond the appearance to the real. One insight realized can forever change your course. Absolutely everything comes from God, Source, Oneness, Life, The All That Is, or whatever you prefer to call it. When we don't perceive what is true, we feel a sense of lack and deficiency. It's just the way it works, have you noticed? We may even conclude our Spirit needs fine-tuning, when Spirit is already whole and complete! Spirit cannot be harmed. Spirit, what you eternally are, is untouched. It's our minds that need the adjustment, because it's the mind that can lead us astray.

Some will say we need to cultivate and enhance the different qualities of our being (that seem dormant) as a way to boost our self-esteem and lessen the impact our imperfections have on us. It's basically a strategy to take our focus off of our perceived imperfections and place it elsewhere. Granted, we often get what we pay attention to, but in this case, we're just rearranging the deck chairs on the Titanic. Compassion, gratitude, integrity, wisdom and humility - innate aspects of who we are - become *objects* in our awareness we seek to amplify. Distraction becomes our method, and creating and maintaining good feelings becomes our primary motive. It's a band-aid approach at best, never getting to the root wound.

While there's nothing wrong with the desire to feel good, it's a contrived and inauthentic strategy. The truth is, we don't have to enhance our inherent *subjective* qualities by paying special attention to them, nor do we need to develop them! This approach takes a LOT of energy - and we're often left feeling like a dog chasing its tail. Paying attention to the effects can get really dizzying; it happens when we don't address the causes. Instead of the direct, rooting out approach, we take the indirect, bypass route, delaying our arrival, sometimes getting lost for a long time. We make it complicated, when all along truth is simple, so simple in fact, that the mind overlooks it.

I'm kind of lazy, and it's not an imperfection. Since I'm usually looking for the most direct route, it comes in real handy sometimes. As a result of a natural inclination towards the path of least resistance, paradoxes have become a very close friend of mine. Once understood, they require no work at all! They're like laser beams, cutting right through the discomfort that illusion brings, like hot butter.

Paradoxically, the qualities we most want to experience arise more than ever as a direct result of rooting out the false. When we see through illusion, when we realize something was never true to begin with, falsehood drops away – and our most desirable qualities *spontaneously* radiate and blossom. Like nature, our spirits are already endowed with perfect qualities that naturally blossom when the proper conditions are prepared.

Seeing what's true is a game of realizing what's already the case, and never about developing skills or improving upon our inherent qualities. Distinguishing truth from falsehood *is* the fertile soil that allows wisdom, peace, self-love and gratitude to bloom. When we seek to cultivate and develop as a method to enhance our qualities (or distract us from negative self-perceptions), we're operating from the dream-state, forever manufacturing our experience. It's inorganic, and we live our lives continually managing our states, endlessly on the wheel of seeking pleasure and avoiding pain. It's a wonderful recipe for staying on an emotional rollercoaster.

All the while, life is in continuous flow, unimpeded - yet we believe we're separate from that flow. There's no such thing as flow *and* us. Oneness isn't just a concept to believe in; it's immediately available as the reality to be realized experientially. If we have any purpose in life, it is this. When we continue to identify with the erroneous perceptions of our minds (that divide and condemn) we remain trapped inside a fiction of our own making - and life inevitably hurts.

When we continue to believe that it actually makes sense to embrace our strengths, while rejecting our weaknesses, we'll never experience the true contentment our hearts long for. Most of us want to love and accept ourselves as we are, and pay it forward, don't we?

The truth is, we're already as worthy as the next person, regardless of our upbringing, intellectual capacity and social standing. And it certainly has nothing to do with how much money you make, how big your house is, or what you look like. At birth, each person is fundamentally endowed with the same intrinsic worth. It sure is a silly notion to think that you accumulate worth over the years based on your achievements or status - or even your value to society, don't you think? Unfortunately, many of us don't realize we're as worthy as the next guy because we've either been told we're not, or *because* of what we tell ourselves. Identified with a mind that compares, contrasts, judges and wishes it was more like others, it's no wonder we often find ourselves in an inner battle.

If we want to be on the receiving end of a spontaneous happiness that needs nothing to be happy, we must see through illusion that hurts and perceive reality as it is, not as we'd like it to be. If we want to possess an authentically healthy self-perception that isn't propped up and sustained by formulas and beliefs, we must work with and understand the law of our experience. Nature doesn't need to improve or foster anything, nor do we. It has no concept of improvement. Only a direct and aware, no-nonsense approach is contained within these pages. Can you handle the truth? I think you can. In fact, I know you can.

This has always been a game of seeing what's already the case. *The Dance of Imperfection - Living in Perfect Harmony with Life* is an in depth re-examination of our interpretations of the concepts we live by, an intimate exploration to clearly see how we've set the rules up in order to live authentically, experiencing the peace, joy and love we are. If we truly are free beings, then it makes sense to really see how we're playing the game of life. We may discover we've set it up only to lose.

Commit to discover like never before, the ways in which we put ourselves behind the eight ball, and identify the rules we've been playing by. If it's appropriate, we can change the rules in our favor and win, not just for ourselves, but also for those around us. No cheating necessary!

Chapter 1
A Perfect Misconception

"To be yourself in a world that is constantly trying to make you something else is a great accomplishment."

~ **Ralph Waldo Emerson**

In the free online dictionary, "imperfection" is defined as *the quality or condition of being imperfect, a fault or defect.* Some of the synonyms included: *flawed, blight, blotch, deformity, blemish, disfigurement, stain, deficiency, inadequate, insufficient and shortcoming.* Some examples of imperfections in a sentence were:

He detected several imperfections in the surface of the jewel. She tried to hide the imperfection in the cloth.

Back in the Elizabethan times, imperfection was defined conceptually as "crack'd in the ring", flawed or imperfect at the perimeter or edge. (It was limited in application to money and artillery). In the early 17th Century, diamond in the rough: *one whose unrefined and external appearance, or ungraceful behavior belies a good or gentle character and untapped potential.*

This expression derives from the disparity between a diamond in its natural state, before being cut and polished, and in its refined state, when it has become an impressive gem. Early Christian writings, especially Paul's, are replete with calls to perfection. Many are from St. Augustine in the Old Testament: *"Thou shalt be perfect with the Lord thy God."* Elsewhere, synonyms for "perfection" are *undefiled, without rebuke, without blemish, blameless, holy and righteous.*

Italy's *Leaning Tower of Pisa* first started out as a concept in the mind of man, unintended to lean after construction. We can find many parallels in our human affairs, and the way humans unintentionally lean towards illusion and not truth. There are several ways we can approach this concept we commonly refer to as "imperfection" - this concept that induces more bouts of depression and lingering insecurity than our current stock market.

One of those ways will be to take a closer look at how we interpret the concept "imperfection" - and some of the implications inherent when we continue to cling to our interpretation. Additionally, we'll look at, and re-examine, the inevitable consequences of *our* tendencies and leanings - and how they inevitably shape our experience.

We'll bring our conceptual interpretations out into the open, unreservedly and with humility - and clearly see, through an earnest willingness to investigate, how our actual perception of the concept "imperfection" manifests itself in our experience. Once we see that, we allow ourselves the opportunity to rework, or reorient ourselves (to the concept) in a way that works for us - if it's necessary for us to do so.

That being said, there *are* actual limitations in our abilities, intellect and emotional makeup that come with the package of being human, and there are *perceived* imperfections in these same areas that aren't based in truth or reality.

The trick is to discern those that are part of our particular makeup, and those that are made up and believed in. To the degree that we give our perceived imperfections attention and energy, to that degree do we also give them credence and continued life. When we give credence to our perceived imperfections, aren't we naturally left feeling vulnerable and insecure? It is this very credence that gives them continued life. Isn't it always our thinking *about* a thing that makes us insecure - and not the actual thing? When we resist and judge those aspects of ourselves that we deem "imperfect," how else *but* insecure can we feel?

We've set ourselves up to lose, but we continue on with the game, hoping to win now and then. Don't we often conclude that *if* we're deficient in a particular area, that it must *then* mean something else? For example, *if* I don't measure up here, *then* I won't be able to successfully perform there? *If* I don't improve on this flaw - or eradicate this flaw, *then* I won't ever be truly happy. Is it our actual weaknesses that cause so much angst, or is it our thinking about our actual weaknesses that causes the angst? Is it possible that our thinking and perceiving is flawed and imperfect?

We tend to overlook that just maybe our perception is the real culprit, habitually leaning towards believing the thoughts in our head to tell us what's true. We pay attention to our perceptions, without considering maybe we'd be better off paying attention to the perceiver - and the validity of the perceptions. Most of our perceived imperfections are, in fact, just that, contrived and made-up notions created in our minds that essentially tell us something shouldn't be the way it is.

We then label that something as "imperfect," or not as we'd like it to be. I say, "contrived" because we have a tendency to, with a glass half-empty paradigm, compare our present character traits, abilities and personality with some imagined ideal, or to someone we wish we were more like.

In other words, we essentially tell ourselves that what we innately possess *shouldn't* be, and that somehow, we don't measure up when we compare ourselves to that ideal, or to another. We fail to recognize that what we're really NOT measuring up to is nothing other than a mind-created fantasy. If pressed, most of us wouldn't even be able to clearly communicate our standard of perfection - or what it looks like! We suffer from our own perceptions, and nothing else. Instead of directly experiencing who we are, *as* we are - we experience our interpretations *about* who we are.

Isn't this the way it works in our experience? If we don't possess the qualities or things we want, don't we conclude we must acquire that quality, and those things? Since most of us are not ultimately content as we are, the search or chase is on. Generally, we unconsciously set it up within ourselves that we won't be content and secure *until* we possess that ideal or state of perfection we imagine will bring us the security and contentment we seek. For some of us, what others naturally possess becomes a threat to us, and we find ourselves in a competition of sorts, covertly hiding what we feel is missing, and overtly compensating for what we feel is lacking.

We go into pretend mode, not living authentically - and with gratitude for the gifts that only we uniquely bring to life. Since our consciousness can basically only focus on one thing at a time, it's easy for us to forget that to deny our actual weaknesses is to deny our very humanity, our unique thumbprint. Due to our egos being somewhat (or mostly) fragile, we don't always want to acknowledge that it is in our shared weaknesses, and not our strengths, where we really connect with others in a meaningful and healing way.

After all, it is our strengths and abilities - and not our weaknesses - that makes us different. Instead, in our arrogance and ignorance, we cling to the ideas that limit us, professing that somehow "God messed up; I shouldn't have these flaws and blemishes - and I'd be happier if I didn't." On some level, we know that what we cling to can only bind us, yet we hold fast to our beliefs that claim what presently is, *can or should* be different than it is right now.

And it's never true, is it? Things are always AS they are, aren't they? They may be different than they *were*, and they may be different than they will be, but they are always as they are - *and can never be presently different than they are.*

Not seeing this simple truth, we hop on the wheel of suffering and tell ourselves a story that goes something like, "If I can figure out how to eradicate these annoying shortcomings, then I'll feel safe and secure in this world. If I can figure that out, then I'll feel good about the way I am - and *then* I'll feel good about contributing to the world and those around me!" We don't yet realize that fully accepting ourselves exactly the way we are *is* the way *to* transcend our insecurity and self-consciousness.

Only when we are able to unequivocally accept the way *we are,* with all our weaknesses - perceived or real, can we accept *others* for the way they are, exactly *as* they are. Sometimes we fool ourselves thinking there must be an easier, softer way. Wisdom sees that this mutuality is real love, the kind that gives just for the sake of giving and asks for nothing in return.

As *they* must, these misguided notions that tell us that we can be intrinsically different than we presently are become obstacles in our awareness. They become the ways in which we hand over our power to something that has no real substance or reality - our contrived and imagined misconceptions that inevitably divide us.

Even though we are already and always whole, as a result of our self-perception, we feel divided. These misguided notions are added layers that get in the way of our ability to show up authentically in the moment. Carrying a heavy burden of misconceptions around, they prevent us from meeting the moment as it is. As *we* must, we inevitably suffer from these delusions and flaws in our thinking, but only every time! Since we can only ever really operate from the way we *see* things, we operate from "perfect misconceptions" that divide and fracture, until we don't anymore.

Until we decide we want something else, like a child put in a timeout for his behavior, we continue to put ourselves in a timeout. If we've literally had enough pain and exhausted ourselves, grace has a way of stepping in - but only if we're ready to accept that grace. No one can make us ready, and grace doesn't force its way in. Grace doesn't operate when we're still holding on. Unless we're willing to hand it over, grace won't step in.

In the meantime, each moment STILL provides a fork in the road, where we can choose to take the same direction as usual, or take the path that's not divisive and hurtful. Despite carrying around our baggage of misconceptions and erroneous interpretations that divide and hurt, each moment is STILL fresh and new. But in order to recognize this, and in order to drop our baggage, we must be acutely aware of our present situation and perspective, don't we?

In order to drop that unnecessary baggage, we must be aware that we're carrying it in the first place. Since we sense that truth only reveals itself when we allow ourselves not to know, we give up our need *to* know what it looks like, and we give up our need *to* know how it will turn out. Wisdom sees that it is the unknown - and not what we "know," where our answer lies, where our freedom is. The known isn't cutting it. Wisdom knows our own being isn't separate from the wisdom of all life.

Thus, with faith and courage, we take the unknown road. Wholly unconcerned, yet intimately engaged, we courageously step into the fire of the unknown, knowing that "the way of perfection" doesn't even exist in this finite, human existence, at least not in the cultural sense we've come to believe in. We see that it exists only in the mind of the one who believes it. Until we see this completely, this layer won't drop away. Fully seen, it drops away.

Language consists of concepts that describe something in particular. If we can really see that the function of language is to describe something else - and not ultimately define that something else, we're facing the right direction. If we see that language is inherently limited, with dividing lines that point to where that *something* seemingly begins and ends, then we give ourselves a chance to transcend our restricting and damaging notions about what it means to be imperfect.

Further, if it has dividing lines, any concept must also imply what it is not. Most importantly, we see it must be dualistic in nature, having an opposite like cold has hot, wet has dry, up has down, pain has pleasure, and left has right.

Hence, all language is dualistic and possesses a seeming opposite. All language is limiting in that the word is never the thing, but only points to that thing. Concepts can only be described in relation to its opposite. If you read my first book, *"Born To Be Happy - How To Uncover Your Natural State of Happiness,"* you might remember I posed the question, "Can you drink the word "water," or be burned by the word, "fire"?" No, of course not. The word is never the actual, and can't ever be the actual. Words are symbols that represent something else. Once this is clearly understood and *seen*, we can then safely conclude that, since the word "water" can't ever quench our thirst, the word "imperfection" isn't the *actual* state of imperfection, either.

Naturally, with every concept having its opposite, we would be remiss if we didn't address the opposite concept called "perfection," wouldn't we? And that the concept "perfection" can't be the actual state or condition of perfection, either, can it? If we really want to understand (and come to *see*) how it is that any concept interpreted can have such great influence in our lives, wouldn't it make sense for us to *really* look into it? I mean, wouldn't that be a worthy endeavor that's deserving of our real and undivided attention? I say YES, wholeheartedly - and I hope you agree.

If the word isn't the actual, then certainly the way in which we *interpret* a defined concept surely isn't the actual, either, is it? It's just our interpretation, right?

As it goes in our experience, we'd have no other alternative than to live and experience *from* that particular interpretation. Have you ever considered that your interpretation and perception of the words *perfection and imperfection* can (and would be) resolutely refuted by so many others? And wouldn't that particular acknowledgement call into question the validity of those interpretations - and the fact that it's a totally subjective thing?

If we really look, we notice that we aren't stretching it when we say that there are as many different ways to perceive a concept, as there are those who perceive that concept! When it comes to something so subjectively interpreted as the concepts, "perfection and imperfection," we see how this is especially so.

Another chief obstacle is our lack of knowledge about the nature of consciousness itself - more specifically, our lack of awareness *(the no-thing that sees)* about the nature of consciousness itself. If we take a look, we can see the incredible rapidity of movement in the moment-to-moment, instant-to-instant processes of our minds.

Faster than a supercomputer analyzing millions upon millions of bits of information, the implications of its rate of speed are far greater than it would acknowledge - and far greater than we might even be *able* to see, and hence, be *able* to acknowledge.

We see that consciousness automatically and spontaneously "chooses" what it deems best in each moment, relative to millions of pieces of data, dominated and influenced by patterns of past conditioning. It's quite obvious to me that the crux of the problem lies in our failure to clearly recognize that the greatest catalyst for conflict (both internal and external) isn't just our spontaneous and ongoing compulsion to evaluate and interpret concepts.

Believing in and identifying with those interpretations as being anything other than a delusional fiction is the main cause of our undoing, and the proverbial nail in the coffin sealing our experience.

Information comes to us second hand, and our descriptions and stories are always (and already) a step behind, describing what already came and went. While we live in the present, our thoughts reflect the past. It's as if we're reading today's newspaper (based on yesterday's events) and we try and nail it down, attempting to make yesterdays events present and relative. It's like trying to fit a square peg in a round hole.

Since absolutely everything is on the move and in flux, we can't ever nail *anything* down, but in our ignorance, we keep trying to grasp what cannot be grasped. And we wonder *why* attachment can be so painful! Desire isn't a problem; attachment *TO* desire is the problem.

Clinging to old news, we tie ourselves down, trying to cling to our own shadow. This is what illusion does, and this is what illusion has *us* do. And all the while, right in the midst of this goose chase, is the wisdom of insecurity that patiently waits for us to see the pure folly of trying to grab hold of what must disappear. Like a loyal and faithful lover, the wisdom of insecurity is always right where we are, gently beckoning us to just let go, reminding us that literally everything is on the move, in flux and never static.

Unconsciously living from our fixed, conceptual interpretations about flowing reality, we remove ourselves from the spontaneous flow and movement of life. Life is dancing one way, and we're dancing in another way. It's like we're dancing the jitterbug and our partner (life) is trying to waltz with us. Consequently, we're out of sync with life and we feel out of balance. Thus, we try and cultivate balance in our lives without ever addressing the source of the problem, our perception. Like the rabid dog's nature is to bite, it is illusion's nature to divide, fracture and hurt.

If we're honest with ourselves, we admit that we crave connection with life and others. If we're honest, we can readily admit that we often fear what we want most. In our fears and ideas about what's "best and right," we erect barriers to that union realized. In union, there's no separation or division.

Without belief in separation, there isn't anything vying for our attention, telling us there's a problem that needs solving. Without any separation, there isn't anything that stands apart from us that *can* give us any problem. It's only when we distance ourselves from anything, push it away or avoid it, does it come back to haunt us.

Without pushing away the opposite experience of the concept we call joy (pain), and without resisting or running from the opposite of what we call courage (fear), both experiences are okay with us because we know how it all works. The only thing that can cause us pain is when we believe our mind's interpretations. Until we *REALLY care about how our lives go,* we get more of what we don't want. Like a heroin addict, we can never get enough of what we don't really want.

Let's look at the evolution and various meanings of the word "perfection" in order to get a broader perspective, shall we? Granted, this book is more about imperfection than perfection, but I hope you see the value in delving a bit further in its opposite, in the hope of gaining a greater understanding of how avoiding or compensating for our perceived imperfections can only divide us.

What is perfection, really? Is it actual or imagined? According to Wikipedia, "The oldest definition of perfection goes back to Aristotle." In the Book *Delta of the Metaphysics*, he distinguishes three meanings for the term, or rather three shades of one meaning, but nonetheless, three different concepts. *That is perfect*:

1. Which is complete - which contains all the requisite parts;
2. Which is so good that nothing of the kind could be better;
3. Which has attained its purpose

Could this early interpretation also point to a way of seeing, as in how the enlightened sages and saints have been attempting to convey for ages? Could this be a way of perceiving that suggests whatever is presently arising is perfectly appropriate *and* complete as it is - and in fact, cannot be other than it is? The Jesuit priest, Anthony de Mello, who went on to really investigate truth and reality in his later years said, "Enlightenment is the *absolute cooperation with the inevitable.*"

One of the chief aims of this book is to delve deeper into this way of seeing, and the real meaning the enlightened were pointing to - and what the enlightened continue to point to today. To Aristotle, *perfect* meant complete with nothing to add or subtract to.

The paradox of perfection - that imperfection or weakness is perfect - applies not only to human affairs, but to technology as well. Irregularity in semiconductor crystals (an imperfection in the form of contaminants) is requisite for the production of semiconductors. In regards to the realm of physics, the physicist designates as a perfectly rigid body, one that "is not deformed by forces applied to it." A crystal is perfect when its physically equivalent walls are equally developed.

However, the expression "perfect" is also used colloquially as a superlative (perfect idiot, perfect scoundrel, perfect storm). Perfectionism has also been construed as that which is best. In theology, when Descartes and Leibniz termed God "perfect", they had in mind something other than *model;* than that which *lacks nothing;* than that *achieves its purpose;* than that fulfills its functions; or than that is *harmonious.*

Along with the idea of perfection, Holy Scripture conveyed doubt as to whether perfection was attainable for man. According to John 1:8, *"If we say that we have no sin, we deceive ourselves and the truth is not in us"* and then goes on to say, *"Perfect love casts out fear."* The Christian doctrine of perfection rests on the Gospel of Matthew 5:48, *"Be ye therefore perfect, even as your Father in heaven is perfect."* Those who believe in a God separate from His creation might say that only He is perfect, and that He wants us to strive for perfection, even when we believe He didn't create us to *be* perfect! Some say that only true love is perfect. Spiritually, perfection is beyond measure, and ineffable.

Spirit is intrinsically whole and complete, while our humanity, consisting of personality, past conditioning and experience, is broken and incomplete. The 17th century philosopher, Benedict Spinoza asserted that there was no personal God, and perfection became a property of (even a synonym for) the existence of reality, or the essence of all things. The 18th century brought a world of change to the idea of moral perfection.

Moving away from religious to secular, perfection was a fundamental article of faith for the Enlightenment. Its central tenet was that indeed, nature was perfect; and perfect, too, was *the man who lived in harmony with nature's law.* Primitive man was held to be the most perfect, for he was closest to nature.

For the ancient philosophers, the essence of perfection had been harmony. The Stoics introduced the concept of perfection into ethics, describing it as harmony - with nature, reason, and man himself. They held that such harmony, such perfection, was attainable for anyone. Cicero wrote in, "On the Nature of the Gods" that:

"The world encompasses within itself all beings, and what could be more nonsensical than denying

perfection to an all-embracing being. Besides the world, there is no thing that does not lack something and that is harmonious, perfect and finished in every respect."

File the above description by Cicero away; we'll be revisiting it in more depth later. For the remainder of this book, let's set aside perfection, relative to the disciplines of physics, chemistry, mathematics, art and even aesthetics. Let's look at it in a much more practical way, a way that directly impacts our human affairs - as it pertains to our very lives.

I can only assume that you're interested in this topic as it pertains to your life - and the way you live your life. Can I safely assume this? If we really *look until we see*, we recognize that perfection is indeed, an idea arbitrarily created and defined by a culture (or individual) that seeks to identify ways to measure one's progress and level of success. In other words, we make it up.

We make up ways to measure how we presently are in relation to where we ultimately want to be. Unfortunately, we often make it up in such a way that works against us and *not* in harmony with the law of our experience. Sadly, it's a concept many of us have erroneously tied into measuring our self-worth, which in turn must directly impact our degree of authentic happiness. Real happiness doesn't come and go based on our circumstance or situation. Only manufactured happiness does.

The reason why our interpretations about perfection have a tendency to be hurtful and divisive is singular in nature, resulting in a domino effect that spreads out into several, if not all aspects of our lives. The reason is because our made up ideas and therefore, interpretations *about* perfection (in regards to living our lives) have no existence in reality! What's real and true is permanent, and must be present 100% of the time … and certainly not something created by the mind.

Hence, in regards to our very lives and the things we strive to attain - whether it's spiritual, emotional, mental, financial or physical in nature, there is no such thing as "perfection" except for the one we give it!

For me, when I really saw this, I felt both relief and a bit of shock. Knowing that for much of my life, I had been fooled into believing that perfection was an *actual* state or condition possible to achieve. I saw how believing in it caused more pain than joy, more stress than peace, and more insecurity than security. Not only did I see this for myself, I saw it in others as well - and saw the negative impact it had on them, too.

I had a sense that believing in the existence of perfection was all so arbitrary and handed down, like the worn out shirt you got from your older sibling. I noticed I couldn't help project my misconceptions onto those around me. Evidently, I wanted to keep the tradition alive by giving out hand me downs, too. Being ultimately ignorant, I had difficulty allowing others to be exactly as they were.

By being in bondage (as a result of my own views), I couldn't help tying up others *with* those views. If we want to hang on to our present interpretation of *perfection*, we certainly have that right. It's our life and we can live it as we wish. But if we ask, "What is my direct experience as a result of the way I view this concept?" Or, "How might my life be different if I viewed it in a way that works for me", we may be inspired to view our situation differently.

Besides, if I can't escape experiencing how I view life, why not work with myself instead of against myself? Alternatively, how might our life be different if we dropped the concept altogether? Would we rather be "right," or be at peace? If we see that we really do make it ALL up, why would we continue to cling to notions that ultimately bind us instead of liberate us? Is it simply because we are afraid of taking responsibility for our life? Do we need to look at a belief in a higher power judging us in some way? If so, is it true?

Can we absolutely (and unequivocally) know it's true - or do we merely believe it's true? Coming to this realization can bring up a whole host and variety of responses, ranging from fear, reluctance and skepticism, to laughter, relief and utter amazement.

I'm certainly not asking you to take my word on any of this. In fact, I hope you don't. I highly recommend that you don't believe a *single* word you read in this book (or *any* other book for that matter) - but rather, find out what is true in your own experience. Until you do, you'll just be living from someone else's notions and experience, and not from your own organic realization where real knowing happens, where real wisdom blooms.

Humanity is meant to include strengths and weaknesses that typically translate as "perfect" and "imperfect." Whatever arbitrary thing we chase after must elude us. It's like our shadow, forever being one step ahead, never to be apprehended. How many of us continue to strive for an imagined state or condition of perfection, without realizing that it is one of the greatest illusions the world has ever known?

Isn't this part of the human condition, being duped into believing there is actually something called "perfection," and it's something we can actually attain? Is there a way we can better define this concept so that it works for us, and not against us - especially since we make it all up anyway? If you don't agree that we make it all up, and that "perfection" is an actual and real condition, what tells you that? Who told you that? Can you prove it?

What makes one person define or perceive perfection in a totally different way than another person, when looking at, creating, or experiencing the same thing? Don't we decide what is perfect, based on our likes, dislikes, preferences and opinions? In a free society that most of us get to enjoy, don't we GET TO decide what's perfect for us? Aren't we essentially the architects of our own lives?

Being that architect, what if we were to simply drop the concept altogether from our blueprint, so that it doesn't manifest and make its way into our finished product, our very life? What would that be like, to live without any concept of "perfection" at all? If we could, wouldn't that, in one fell swoop, wipe out "imperfection" as an actual condition, too? Wouldn't that be liberating for us?

Assuming one could reach a state or condition of perfection in any endeavor one chooses, how would one even know when they reached it? If they did know when they reached it, what would they do - celebrate the attainment by hanging up "their perfection shingle" outside their homes, proclaiming to the world that they finally arrived? How boring would that become? Won't the novelty and satisfaction of that state or condition fade away, just like everything else must?

What if, instead, we saw everything already perfect, as it is? That the attainment was in our seeing and perceiving - and was already a done deal? What would that be like?

There's a poignant story from the Zen tradition you may have heard of. *There was a man of great stature in Japan who had a beautiful home, and a garden with such beauty that it would take your breath away upon seeing it. The centerpiece of the garden was a large beautiful tree.*

It was late autumn and the leaves were dying. One day the man learned that he was going to be visited by a number of government dignitaries – something that rarely happens, even to people of great status. He ordered all the servants in his home to prepare his home for the arrival of his guests. There were only three days before they arrived, and there was much to do.

The man insisted that while his servants focused on preparing the home and the meal, he would personally tend to the garden – his pride and joy. The man pruned every tree and bush with great attention to detail. He then proceeded to rake every leaf from the ground, until every single leaf was removed. Now, next to the man's home was a Zendo. One day, as the man was raking the leaves in his yard he noticed one of the Zendo's Masters watching him from one of the balconies. As a matter of fact, the Zen Master would appear on the balcony at the exact time the man would begin working on his yard each day.

He would sit and watch the man all day without saying anything. As the man would go into his home after working, so too, would the Zen Master leave the balcony and retreat inside. The man noticed this, and even took pride in the fact that the Master never corrected him.

Surely, he would correct me if I were not doing something in a less than perfect manner, he reasoned. So when the last day came and the man picked up the last leaf on the ground, he looked up over at the Master and said, "What do you think of my garden, isn't it beautiful?" Smiling, the Zen Master took a few minutes to look over the garden from the balcony. "The garden is very beautiful, but there is something missing."

The man suddenly became very concerned as his guests were arriving shortly. "What is it, Master … what's missing, can you please assist me?" At the man's request, the Zen Master came down from the balcony and walked over into the man's garden. He looked around again, and after a while said, "Ah, I know what it is." The Zen Master walked over to the large tree at the center of the yard and shook it several times, until leaves began falling from the tree, covering the grounds of the garden. The Zen Master looked at the man with a smile and said, "That's what it needed – now it looks perfect."

Chapter 2
A Level Playing Field

"And I will show you that there is no imperfection in the present, and can be none in the future, And I will show that whatever happens to anybody it may be turn'd to beautiful results, And I will show that nothing can happen more beautiful than death, And I will thread a thread through my poems that time and events are compact, And that all the things of the universe are perfect miracles, each as profound as any."

~ **Walt Whitman** (The Leaves of Grass)

Whitman is one of my favorite enlightened people because of his remarkable ability to eloquently point to Truth by using the written word, usually in the form of poetry and prose. There is something in the above quote, that is the crux of this chapter - and in fact, that *something* is the thread that weaves throughout the entirety of this book.

Admittedly, I am wondering if you were alerted to this "something" in the first chapter. Remember we said that all language is both dualistic in nature, limiting in the sense that the word is never the thing, nor does it define that thing, but only points to that thing? In fact, it can only be described in relation to its inherent opposite?

We also said that, in terms of our daily human affairs, that "perfection" isn't something that actually exists in reality, other than the arbitrary meaning we give it? In other words, without referencing thought, the concept has no reality. Well, if this is true, then its opposite must not exist, either! And so, the concept "imperfection" then, as it pertains to our human affairs, has no existence in reality other than the one we give it. We see that the belief in the existence of imperfection is rooted in wanting the moment to be other than it is.

Belief in the existence of imperfection is the same thing as saying, "This person is lacking," or "This moment is lacking." And it's never true. Belief in the existence of imperfection is tantamount to saying, "Humanity (as God or Source created it) should not have been designed this way - with both strengths and weaknesses." As Walt Whitman aptly stated, *"there is no imperfection in the present and can be none in the future, and I will show that whatever happens to anybody can be turn'd to beautiful results."* If you were hoping to learn a different perspective on the popularly accepted assumption that imperfection is indeed an actual state or condition in reality, I'm sorry to disappoint you. I'm sorry to break it to you, but there's no such thing - and there never was!

It's like the mirage in the desert that appears to be real; it appears to be moving, but once you walk directly up to it to get a close look, it disappears. It disappears because it was never there to begin with; it only appeared to be there. On the other hand, if you came with an open heart and mind, I invite you to stick with me here. In time, hopefully you'll see the truth in the declaration that *perfection and imperfection* are concepts that have no existence in reality other than the one we give it.

If it only exists in our minds, it isn't real. Actually, we can say this about any concept. *As it pertains to our human affairs, what the concept imperfection points to isn't an actual condition in reality.* There is nothing lacking and there isn't anything in the universe that shouldn't be the way it is. That said, how *can* imperfection be a reality?

In other words, its existence is manufactured, sustained and maintained in the minds of those who continue to believe in its reality, whatever the reason or payoff happens to be. Personally, I don't really ever utter the word *imperfection* - not just because I'm afraid to give it life, but because I know that it's no more real than the Loch Ness monster. As a result, I don't really have a sense of it, either. However, I do have a real and organic sense of "perfection" that isn't a result of any interpreted concept - and I see it absolutely everywhere I look. Because I see it everywhere, this sense of perfection has no opposite.

I'm aware this may seem like a contradiction. Whenever we try to comprehend things with the mind, contradictions appear to exist. However, this isn't a book intended for your mind. It's intended for YOU. As each chapter builds on the previous one, hopefully this point will become crystal clear. Since mind's function is to compare, contrast, evaluate, judge and maintain preferences, experiences will arise (or be called on) that aren't preferred or desired. If a situation calls for us to utilize and express our weaker abilities, we're not always thrilled to do so.

One day we'll see that, without any labels or descriptions, without being attached to preferences and outcomes, direct experience is radically different, and certainly more pleasurable. Without distinguishing imperfect from perfect, we notice that it is just energy moving through - and it's not a problem.

I must confess, before I sat down to actually write this book, a short conversation arose within that went something like, "Maybe the best way to write about imperfection would be the way the vast majority have already done and continue to do - and in line with how our culture views this topic. That way, you'd be appealing to the masses, giving them what they expect, generating the most attention - and people would certainly 'get it' and understand where you're coming from.

You could follow the same trodden path, and approach it as if it's an actual state or condition, and comfort the reader by encouraging them to accept 'the perfection of imperfection,' because after all, we're all beautiful train wrecks with a shared destination, right? Besides, flaws, deficiencies and inadequacies are part of the package of being human, and God doesn't make junk! We're all 'perfectly imperfect,' and there's great consolation in this fact!" Perhaps provide some dynamic time-bound, powerful tools and strategies (including reframing and mirroring) to better negotiate and live amidst these conceptual anchors that drag us down, and keeps us immobile.

Well, I just couldn't do it. Something wouldn't let me. As I contemplated this softening, cliché-laden approach for about a whole two seconds, I knew that I just couldn't bring myself to add to all the misunderstanding surrounding these two concepts that wreaks so much havoc in the lives of so many good people. In fact, there are mountains of it all over the place, giving it further life. Sadly, some of it is intentional, irresponsible and self-serving. We certainly don't need more untruths piling up; there's more than enough already. In fact, we're knee deep in it, and frankly, it stinks! Besides, I'd just be lying, and I won't do that. It would be paramount to slaying just one head of the hydra, only to watch multiple heads grow back.

In truth, aside from food, air, water and shelter, we don't "need" a thing. There's no outside agency, there's no-thing external that insists or needs for us to see *anything* in particular, or to be any other way than we already are. Nevertheless - relatively speaking, in the hope of living a more contented life, we *can see what's real* and replace false ideas with ideas that point towards freedom. That's what this book is intended to do. Truth must be present all the time. Being 100% present all the time, what's true never comes and goes; it never leaves us. Through conditioning or "past" experience, we may have believed or felt otherwise, but truth is always right where we are.

It can only *be* right where we are, despite any appearance to the contrary. It's eternally available and present, right here, right now. If a concept truly just points to, and isn't the actual, what we *need* is more accurate pointing - pointing in the direction of Truth, and not in the direction of illusion that fractures. While the truth cannot be contained within this or *any* other book, the concepts or words you read here are intended to point you in the direction of truth, so that it can be revealed to you.

You won't find any band-aid approaches, end around or bypassing approaches here. Rest assured that this is a direct and immediate approach that doesn't involve a process or method – or the need to "cultivate" anything. Processes and methods have a beginning, middle and an end, and an unstable life span; it would be geared for your mind to try and "get" or understand.

While your mind may conceptually understand these methods, *you* wouldn't be freed from whatever the affliction is that ails you. What needs to be seen isn't anything the mind *can* see. Again, I'd just be re-arranging the deck chairs on The Titanic. All *methods that require time are for the mind, and since they're* rooted in illusion and not reality, any benefit can't last. Since it doesn't last, it isn't real. Since it isn't real, it must inevitably hurt. YOU don't need any "time" to see this. You can see this immediately, right now.

You *will* find an intensive, DIRECT and practical approach here (that can work for you) if you resist the popular way of looking with the mind. If you are totally confused right now, don't worry. Remain open and curious, with an earnest desire to really look until you see. If you allow the words to sink into your heart that already knows, a whole new experience can arise for you. If you find yourself looking and agreeing, disagreeing, evaluating, comparing, judging or resisting, you can be sure you're looking with your mind. If it's truth you're after, mind ultimately isn't the most useful tool for the job. Granted, it *can* be useful in many instances, but not for realizing truth, or for freeing ourselves from what ails us.

In fact, most of the time, and in most instances, our minds are an obstacle to seeing what's true. In my book, *"When Wisdom Blooms – Awaken The Sage Within,"* I discussed how to know when we're looking with the heart as opposed to the mind. If you haven't read it yet, I will repeat it here: If ever we find ourselves looking with an intense curiosity that has no expectation of finding anything in particular, non-judgmentally and without any bias from the mind, we can be sure that's a good indicator we're looking with the heart. If we find that we are in an *open state of discovery* where we aren't evaluating what we're looking at in relation to the past, we can be sure we are looking from the heart, from our innate wisdom that resides below the neck.

Like a highly skilled and precise surgeon, we'll get to the root wound that still hurts and shine a light on it in order to get a real good look at it. In order to really examine anything, we need to look closely. The better the look we get, the more we can see it for what it really is. The closer we get to it, the more we'll be able to hear its voice. If we ask it what its story is, it will tell us. It's pretty open that way. We will look at and undress the old dressing (our interpretation of and belief in the concepts perfection and imperfection) and find out whether it's healed or not. If it isn't healed - if it's still an open wound, we can clean it and apply the proper cure that lasts until we do.

Truth seen (and taken up) is that cure, and once applied, it never needs to be cleaned or removed. Therefore, it doesn't need any new and sterile dressing, either. In fact, we're done dressing up the dream state! We'll re-examine what we *think* we know, re-examine all we've been told in school, in church or in any book, not just in regards to the concepts "imperfection and perfection", but absolutely everything we cling to, including ourselves. Innocently and without bias, looking in the direction where Truth can be revealed is our practice.

If you find some of the pointers repetitive or even redundant, it's for a reason. If you find some (or even many of the words you read here) paradoxical and contradictory, it's for a reason - and not a result of a confused author. Language is already filled with paradoxical statements and seeming contradictions. Using language that points to truth and freedom - and away from illusion, is even MORE FRAUGHT with seeming contradictions. If there is only one point in this entire book where I ask you to just "trust me on this," it would be this point - that is, until you see this for yourself. The use of language naturally involves paradox and invites contradiction.

In essence, life is paradoxical and often contradictory. Whitman said, *"Do I contradict myself? Very well, then, I contradict myself. I am large and contain multitudes."* I love that quote. Not just because it illustrates my point here, but more importantly, it speaks to our essential nature as both human and spirit simultaneously, one without any separation. It speaks to both our limited and unlimited nature, to both our confused and clear nature. Never being just one thing, everything is connected - and despite any appearance, nothing is separate in reality.

Things can be both something and *not* that something simultaneously. Most people are free, but enslaved at the same time. Everyone is alive and dying at the same time.

So, like all words, the words and ideas presented here *point to* a greater and infinite reality, an all-encompassing reality that envelops both our limited mental and intellectual capacity, and our infinite spirit nature. This all-encompassing reality is larger than any conceptual framework we can come up with; it's larger than anything our minds can comprehend. Really *seeing* this, we do well to let the words penetrate more in our hearts than of our minds, where Truth never is found or realized.

The mind, being a finite thing, can never apprehend or understand the infinite, no matter how hard it tries, regardless of its approach. How can the mind (while a wonderful and useful tool, more powerful than any man-made supercomputer) understand that which produced it?

How can something finite with a particular shelf life - and will die with the body - possibly understand or comprehend the infinite source that created *it?* How can the finite mind, bound by time, understand or comprehend that which is timelessly prior, beneath and behind it? How can the mind comprehend that which encompasses it? It can't, but we endlessly try - with the mind! How's that for ironic?

Now, if you don't presently see this, then I imagine this may be confusing, but does that mean it isn't true? Does it mean you won't ever see this? Heck no. Let me rephrase that: If you continue to look with the mind, you won't see this. Haven't there been times where you read something, or saw a movie a second time, and it finally penetrated in a way it didn't before?

Can I ask you a question? Are you the mind, or do you *have* a mind? If you say you are the mind, then I'd ask, "If you can notice the mind thinking, how can you *be* the mind? Wouldn't you have to be prior to the mind in order to notice it? What's aware of the mind?" *Hint*: it's not mind. It may appear that I'm getting off topic, but it's all tied in and non-separate. One thing greatly affects the other. Rest assured that I'm not going off on a tangent; there aren't any wild goose chases here. There's been far too many of them already. Besides, if you really *see* that you are not the mind, that you are the aware spirit presence prior to the mind, this whole issue of perfection vs. imperfection becomes a moot point!

You'd no longer identify yourself *as* the mind - and your identity with everything the mind latches onto would drop away. The ballgame would be over, and you'd be free from any concept, free from mind and emotion. Granted, you'd still feel and think, but you'd no longer be attached to these energies, and therefore, you couldn't suffer. There would be a spontaneous shift in identity (when it's "meant" to happen) as a result of seeing what's actually true.

You'd see that it's the mind - and not YOU, that latches onto concepts and believes in them in order to feel safe and secure. YOU don't need this security; YOU already *are* this security. As long as we continue to identify with our mind - as our real identity, it won't be seen. If this is confusing, notice that your awareness of confusion isn't confused at all.

There are many well-intentioned people who are unknowingly disseminating erroneous information to those who sorely want the kind of freedom that liberates. How many of us want short-term fixes to what's ailing us? Don't we really want permanent and lasting solutions to our problems and challenges? Yes, most of us do, but most of us won't ever do whatever it takes, either. And that's okay, too. No one is saying you "should" want it more than anything - and if they do, they're delusional. To those who want freedom at any cost, nothing less than the real thing will do. In the guise of wanting freedom, whether we admit it or not, some of us just want to be entertained and distracted from our lives. And that's okay, too ... until it isn't anymore. Only you can know what your real intention is.

So why aren't most of us getting what we really need, if we really want it? For one, we aren't listening to the "right" people! This isn't a judgment by the way; it's simply an observation. We must be aware and vigilant as to whom we go to for solutions. Nothing so big to see, is it? I'm not going to go to a homeless guy on the street for financial advice, am I? Would I go to someone very obese for my fitness and nutrition goals? No, I wouldn't. For the most part, we just aren't receiving the most accurate pointers from these unqualified sources. Like a domino effect, they end up simply passing along what's been handed down to them, without ever really validating their assertions for themselves. If it hasn't been realized experientially - and it doesn't come and go, then they only have conceptual knowledge.

With all the familiar clichés, buzz-words and catchy phrases out there, it can make a lot of sense to the mind. Since it sounds very reasonable, and *seems* logical to our minds, we conclude it must be right and true. We reason that since so many other good and intelligent people believe it, that it must be right! In so doing, we further sustain the illusion we actually want to see through. We unsuspectingly read concepts and look in directions (from other unsuspecting, well-intended people) where truth won't ever reveal itself. It's here, and it's not hidden, but we're not being properly pointed. The good news is, we *can know* if we're facing the right direction just by the byproducts of looking in a particular direction.

What is our experience as a result of looking in that direction and following the pointers of that particular individual? Does harmony and being in the flow last - or is it short-lived and fleeting? The proof is in the pudding, and our direct experience *is* that pudding. We can't fool ourselves, nor can we escape ourselves. Do we have more clarity or less clarity? Does doubt arise often? Have our previous insecurities significantly alleviated, or have they been removed as a result of the new perception? Are we still negotiating with life and/or spending a lot of energy on managing our states?

Unfortunately, most of these message bearers neglected to look and see whether their realizations have stabilized - and that the fruits don't come and go, before pointing others. Personally, I just wouldn't feel right perpetuating the dream state, because in truth, there's SO MUCH of that already going on – for centuries. That's exactly what I'd be doing if I went the popular and familiar route. Injecting illusion only spreads further illusion.

As life begets more life, so too, does illusion beget more illusion. Giving further credence to these concepts isn't necessary. In fact, giving further validity to these concepts is harming. No pat on the back deserved for me; I'm simply suggesting that, in addition to going within, that it's vital we notice *where* we go for guidance when we go outside of ourselves.

Where we go makes a huge difference actually, and is usually the difference between seeing and not seeing – and what comes with that seeing or not seeing. There's a felt and shared sense of responsibility that comes along with realizing the truth of something. I had to tell the truth because that's what integrity insists on doing. When we don't do what integrity insists, we feel some degree of angst. Therefore, I knew this (couldn't or wouldn't be a book) about making the reader feel better about their "imperfections" by simply accepting them, or about giving them alternate ways and strategies to cope with their own perceived flaws. The byproducts aren't lasting or useful – at least not in a practical way that serves long term.

This is about telling the truth, and having the courage to face our so-called deficiencies and inadequacies. This is about investigating them, instead of blindly believing in them, just because someone else said so. This is about inviting you to consider the very real possibility that through no fault of your own, perhaps you've been looking in directions where truth won't ever be revealed. This is an invitation to look in directions you may not be accustomed to looking. It may not always *feel* good, and you may experience varying degrees of fear, reluctance and other uncomfortable feelings, but so what? Sometimes truth and feeling good don't always go together. Yeah, and? Don't let feelings stop you - they're just energy anyway.

If feeling good is more important to us than realizing what's true - and enjoying the immense benefit from that - then there's a very good chance we're going to bail when it doesn't feel so good.

As we already know, because we've experienced it many times, sometimes the truth hurts. Let's not pretend otherwise, and be open to HOWEVER it shows up. If we stick with it, and make no demands of it, and look until we see, we'll notice the seeing is often the letting go. Isn't freedom *from* our minds and emotions what we really want? Don't we really just want to be okay with all of who we are, without being tormented by our own thoughts and opinions we have of ourselves? Haven't the most challenging situations in our lives typically led to the most learning and growth?

If there ever was a state called perfection - where, as Aristotle proclaimed, *"a completeness containing all the requisite parts, where it's so good that nothing of the kind can be any better,"* this is it. It's found in the perception of true seeing. This is my reality - and it has absolutely nothing to do with resignation or complacency. Anyone who knows me knows I'm no doormat. This perception sets us free, once and for all. No maintenance needed. And no, it doesn't "kill" your drive or motivation.

If this beckons you, please read on. I am very aware that just because you're reading this doesn't equate to you buying into it, at least not right now. Actually, I don't want you to "buy into it"... I don't want you to buy into anything here. I want you to *see* it for yourself, in your own experience, beyond belief. Belief isn't required and belief isn't necessary.

Nothing less can, or will, liberate you. There *is* an inescapable integrity required for one to be free; he or she must see for him or herself, without relying on belief or any outside source. This includes the most commonly accepted "authoritative sources" we can ever find. If you do see the truth of this now, that's wonderful, and I hope that in this seeing, you experience as much or more relief and laughter as I did. To suddenly realize that it was all a "crock of you know what" was instantly liberating.

Seeing through the illusory concept called "imperfection" to the reality of its eternal nonexistence, a dropping away (or a dismantlement in the belief) happened of its own accord. It's as if we're rewarded for our willingness to see what's true. Not only did this seeing significantly impact the way I showed up in the present, but also for the way I viewed my so-called past. Knowing that *how absolutely everything unfolded* couldn't have unfolded any other way than it did - and in the manner it did - dissolved *any* leftover regret, guilt, shame and sorrow. If it couldn't have unfolded any other way than it did (and it was only my mind that said otherwise) why would I beat myself up for the things I did?

Why would I create and hold onto a limiting story that said, "It was *because* of my shortcomings that I messed up, or it was due to my flaws that I treated myself or another that way, etc.?" You can imagine the impact this had on how I viewed others as well, and the perceived things that were "done to me". I couldn't fully comprehend that all that stuff, all those negative experiences were still harbored and being carried around for years. I didn't see how believing in untruths significantly influenced how I met the moment.

"Oh, what a tangled web we weave, when we first practice to deceive." This web we've fashioned, literally over a lifetime, seems and feels so real. And since it feels so real, we conclude that it must be real. It may *seem* insurmountable, like climbing Mount Everest, without the aid of oxygen. It may *seem* impossible to find our way out of this deluded and sticky web we've created, but we don't stop at appearances.

Take heart, there *is* a way out. The way out is the way in; the way out isn't to eradicate the web or destroy the web. The way out is to see through the hypnotic web as being unreal, and without a shred of truth in it.

It's about looking beyond appearances to the underlying essence beneath and behind. *See* that the mind's function is to create problems, only to try and solve them. Then, and only then, will the web begin to fall apart and free us from its hold, revealing its true nature, nothing but illusion - through and through. I didn't fully see the direct relationship between how I felt about myself, and how I treated others. I had little appreciation for the fact that all that unresolved "stuff" was still alive in me - in the recesses of my mind, my DNA, my memory … and ultimately, in every fiber of my being.

Like a veil lifted, now I could see. There wasn't anything between myself and what arose … no stories, no agenda, just this and nothing else.

Finally *seeing* that there was no such state or condition called "perfection" allowed me to live without any felt sense of insecurity, psychological or emotional fear. Gone was any regard of "doing it right" or "messing up," because *how* I showed up - the manner in which I showed up, was already taken care of. How I showed up "before" and how I showed up now, was exactly the way I was *meant* to show up. All the energy that would have previously gone towards being concerned about screwing up or being embarrassed was transferred to just being in the moment.

No longer identified with the contents of the mind, there was an organic sense of transparency experienced. If you slung arrows of criticism at me, they wouldn't stick. They still don't. They'd go right through me, landing somewhere beyond me. Being energy without a fixed reference point, there was nothing solid for the arrow to land. What I am is eternally unharmed and untouched - and it has absolutely nothing to do with belief. If something happened that wasn't of my preference, it's okay. If something didn't pan out because of a particular inability or weakness on my part, it's okay. There's always another opportunity, and I noticed that any attachment I had to being "perfect" or insecure about my "imperfections" was gone.

I no longer label things as perfect or imperfect. Things are just as they are. It's really that simple - so simple that I hope you resist the urge to dismiss it. If I can see, so can you. And if you think that *this* is just some strategy or method to soften or alleviate your experience of your interpretations, I won't try and convince you otherwise. I may, however, suggest suspending your judgment until you look and see for yourself – but no one is saying you have to. You may want to hold onto the status quo for whatever reason. Granted, at times, I still strive to get something just right (dare I say perfect) but I don't identify with it or get caught up in it anymore. The end result is just fine by me. Besides, maybe I'll do better next time.

Either way, even though I'm not separate from my creations, they don't define me one bit. This moment is whole and complete, as it is, where all the requisite parts are included, because in fact, it couldn't be any other way than it is. Nothing needs to be added, and nothing needs to be subtracted, except in the mind that says otherwise. Since it was truly seen here, my mind no longer says otherwise. All along it was just a thought believed in. Since I was totally willing to really see for myself, something or no-thing (call it God if you prefer) allowed me to see. You have this very same ability. We all play on a level playing field.

We are all essentially the same, possessing the same faculties of attention and awareness, with the ability to discern what's true and what isn't. Aside from those with significant mental disorders and the like, we really *do play* on even ground. Regardless of our conditioning or past experience, we've all been endowed with the ability to live from truth, not illusion.

No one person is more worthy or deserving of seeing this than another. No one person is better or more worthy than another, from the homeless man in the inner city, to the King of England. I do have deep compassion for those who've had rough and traumatic upbringings, where all kinds of abuse were considered "normal". If this was your case, you never deserved any of that, and absolutely none of it was your fault. As you are right now, you are perfect and complete, without imperfection or inadequacy.

That doesn't mean to walk around thinking you're God's gift to humanity, either. The fact is, we're all intrinsically the same, no better or worse than another. Stop believing your mind that may tell you a different story. It just isn't true. Stop concluding that because you still *feel* it in your bones, in your DNA and in your being, that it must be true. Of course it's still there - it's there because you still believe it to be real. There's great momentum in belief and illusion; it is a very powerful force. Your belief in its existence *is* the energy that gives it life. It really does have that power.

Most importantly, keep looking until you really see, because you can never know when it might happen. And when it does, tell me what you really think about these concepts called perfection and imperfection, okay? Can an eye that sees faultlessly find imperfection?

Whether or not you believe in the existence of imperfection, feel trapped within the sense of imperfection as a reality, to follow is a wonderful, little story …

A water bearer in China had two large pots, each hung on the ends of a pole that he carried across his neck. One of the pots had a crack in it, while the other pot was perfect and always delivered a full portion of water. At the end of the long walk from the stream to the house, the cracked pot arrived only half full. For a full two years this went on daily, with the man delivering only one and a half pots full of water to his house. The perfect pot without the crack was proud of his accomplishments, always delivering a full pot of water. The cracked pot was ashamed and miserable that it was only able to accomplish half of what it was designed to do. After two years of what it perceived as bitter failure, it spoke to the water bearer one day at the stream.

"I am ashamed of myself and because this crack in my side causes water to leak out all the way back to your house." The bearer said to the pot, "Did you notice that there were flowers only on your side of the path, but not on the other pot's side? That's because I have always known about your flaw, and I planted flower seeds on your side of the path, and every day while we walk back, you've watered them. For two years I have been able to pick these beautiful

flowers to decorate the table. Without you being just the way you are, there would not be this beauty to grace my house."

Chapter 3
An Existential Discomfort

"Please, Doc -- nothing too aggressive. I'm kind of attached to my symptoms."

"Striving for excellence motivates you; striving for perfection demoralizes you."

~ Harriet Braiker

Growing up, I can remember being a perfectionist. In sports, I not only had to beat you, I had to do it convincingly. I'd settle for squeaking out a win, but I much preferred to win outright. It was the ego stroke I apparently needed. Losing to my older brothers on our backyard basketball court likely had something to do with this compulsion. In the third grade, I remember being involved in the SRA reading comprehension testing with my fellow classmates. We had to read stories from laminated cards that we'd get from a box on the teacher's desk at the front of the room.

After reading stories, we'd answer questions to test our comprehension level. It really wasn't a competition, but I made it one. In a classroom of over 35 kids, it was you against me for the right to claim the prize of "The Best and Fastest Reader With Great Comprehension Skills!" You won by being faster than the rest of the students. Funny thing is, the girls didn't seem to care about competing. Even at such a young age, the girls had it right! Anyway, I decided that I won if I finished in the top two. You always knew who finished in the top two, because once you finished a lesson, you'd have to get out of your chair and walk up to the front of the room to get a new card.

I still remember watching my friend, Steve, head to the front of the class. He made sure you knew it, too. He'd bang his chair when he got up letting you know he finished before you. I could tell Steve viewed it as a competition, too. I can still remember the jealous feeling, watching him and another kid saunter up to the front. Obviously, this wasn't acceptable to me, so I made some minor "adjustments" in my approach. I started skimming certain sections in order to finish in the top two - and it worked. Aside from the teacher, no one would know my actual scores, so that wasn't a concern; finishing first and winning was.

When it came to playing board games at home with my siblings, I just had to win. Coming from a family of six children, there was a palpable sense of competition in the air. Being the youngest of three boys and being the second to youngest, I can assure you that I got my fair share of beat downs and humiliations that only the youngest in the family can identify with. But my saving grace was that I had a sister, three years younger. Annemarie would unsuspectingly become my prey, allowing me to be in the "w" column most of the time.

In the spirit of full-disclosure, I must admit that whenever I found myself behind, or close to losing in chess, checkers, backgammon, monopoly or battleship, I'd sometimes cheat when she wasn't looking - or when she had to suddenly leave for a bathroom break. I just couldn't stand to hear the words, "You sunk my battleship" ... "King me" ... or "Pass go, give me $200!" And all because I had to win - no matter what it took. Looking back with the benefit of hindsight, it was all because I'd go to any lengths to avoid that feeling of losing. More accurately, I sought to avoid what I told *myself* after I lost.

I hated confirming what I was feeling inside ... that I was insecure, imperfect and flawed, so winning was a way to minimize this sense. There was occasion that I'd lose ... mostly due to the fact my little sister never took her eyes off me and got "lucky!" Over time, she became wise to my ways. Now mind you, I didn't resort to cheating all the time. Nevertheless, it's amazing that at such a young age, the need to win was so strong. I was even desperate to the point I was willing to compromise my integrity to avoid hearing the voice inside reminding me of my inadequacies.

Many of us have a strong inner critic, and we believe what it says to us. As children, we believed it when our parents told us, "You're not a good listener." "Why can't you pay attention when I tell you to do something?" "Why can't you get good grades like your older brother?" "If you don't get your act together, you'll amount to nothing!" They may tell you it's "constructive criticism" and that it's meant to help you. Consequently, the implication was that you shouldn't be bothered by it! Most parents don't intentionally want to hurt us, however, the effects aren't always so good.

Hearing criticism from the outside only compounds what we hear and feel from the inside. And what we do to ourselves, we do to others. In our own blame and shame, we blame and shame others.

Then, we often make the conclusion we're not good enough, worthy enough, and deserving enough.

We tie our behaviors and achievements (or lack of achievements) to our self-worth and become concerned with making mistakes and messing up. We worry about what others think of us, and put a lot of energy into projecting an image of someone who really has it all together. We put on a happy face, never addressing the root wound. Coming to believe we are our behaviors and achievements, our self-esteem and relationships suffer. We continue to beat ourselves up, thinking it's a good strategy to improve who we are, when the opposite is true.

While we continue to experience stress, anxiety, sadness and low energy from believing the criticisms in our head, the option to recognize none of it is true waits to be seen. The option to experience ease of being, peace, happiness and increased energy is instantly available when we align ourselves with what's true.

We live in a culture that's increasingly obsessed with winning and perfection - and actively avoiding, downplaying and hiding "imperfections". Rarely is it about "how you play the game" anymore. Winning is what really matters, and winning in a dominating fashion is a bonus, one sure to get you all kinds of praise and adulation from your peers. It's the icing on the cake, the icing that ensures the envy of your fellow competitors. It's the layer of icing that validates the child's need to cover up his felt sense of lack and insecurity. There's nothing wrong with our kids being involved in playing competitive sports and making a real commitment to one or more.

However, when it becomes so intense that the coaches of our children are pacing up and down the sidelines, yelling at the referees to make the "right" call, or aggressively telling our kids how to "do it the right way" ... something has gone awry and our priorities need to be looked at. When the parents are screaming at the referees and umpires from the bleachers - and fighting with each other - something isn't right. This behavior even goes on with our five and six year olds playing! It's both comical and disconcerting.

More and more, our kids are suffering from the effects of such intense competition. The underlying message is that perfection is an attainable goal and it's your duty to achieve it. Sadly, this pressure on our youth is spilling out in a variety of ways. What was once a healthy outlet to compete and be social is now an intensely competitive avenue for kids to try and validate themselves and make their parents proud. It's manifested as the 12-year old traveling all over, staying overnight in hotels and playing in all kinds of tournaments in various organizations. Practicing 3-6 hours a day between games, sometimes with a personal trainer, isn't uncommon. No wonder so many kids are on medications these days.

I recently read an article online from the New York Times called, *"Risky Rise of Good-grade Pills: Strained students increasingly take stimulants to study and take tests to get into the top schools."* It went on to report that before getting out of his car in the morning to enter school, a particular boy would twist open a capsule of orange powder and arrange it in a neat line on the armrest console. He leaned over, closed one nostril and snorted it. Throughout the parking lot, he said, eight of his friends were all doing the same thing.

The drug wasn't cocaine or heroin, but Adderall, an amphetamine prescribed for attention deficit hyperactivity disorder. The boy said he and his friends routinely shared the drug to study late into the night, focus during tests, and ultimately get the grades worthy of being admitted to the high end, prestigious colleges and universities. The drug did more than jolt them awake for the early morning SAT tests; it gave them laser focus, tailor-made for the marathon of tests long known to make or break college applications. "Everyone in school either has a prescription or has a friend who does," the boy said.

At high schools across the United States, pressure over grades and competition for college admissions are encouraging students to abuse prescription stimulants. Forty students agreed to share their experience as long as they remained anonymous. Each of them emphasized that the drugs were not intended for getting high, but to work harder and meet the ever-rising academic pressures and expectations. We can only imagine where this drug use has led.

In this age of instant gratification and instant news and information, advertisers and media play a significant role in mirroring back our obsession with projecting the right image, wearing the right clothes, driving the right cars, living in the perfect home in an upscale neighborhood. You know, a huge mansion that's a few square feet less than the property it sits on, with the most expensive marble countertops, kitchen cabinets and appliances? The next-door neighbor's bedroom window is twenty feet away … with the perfect spouse raising perfect families - like the Brady Bunch! In a nutshell, the aim is to project the right and perfect life, the kind that's the envy of others.

The goal is to make others want what you have in order to feel validated. Sadly, if we are honest, many of us admit to a degree of feeling content, but also to a superficial kind of satisfaction that ultimately leaves us empty inside. An insecurity regarding *being* that right kind of spouse, parent and friend, isn't that uncommon. Headlines in the magazines and papers on the newsstands, supermarkets and internet invariably convey the same message: dress like this and project this kind of image, hang out with these type of people, drive these cars and do your hair like this person and you too, can be perfect.

The faces and bodies of the people gracing the covers are perfect, but conveniently left out is the airbrushing and other various manipulations applied to make them appear that way. And since you aren't perfect right now, you must buy this magazine or product in order to learn how to be perfect! We really can't place the blame on any one entity. We're all complicit and it spreads like an insidious, infectious disease without any antidote. This seductive message that promises lasting happiness and fulfillment in perfection is sucking us all in. All the while, we have the antidote: it's called integrity and choice.

There is presently an epidemic of eating disorders like bulimia and anorexia that plagues our culture like never before. They are often the result of an obsession to be perfect, or to hide imperfection. Granted, past trauma can and often plays a significant role as well. Since I am not an expert in this area, I won't pretend to know all the particulars of these unfortunate disorders. Certainly, there are numerous factors involved and each case is different. However, not many would argue that an underlying impulse to be perfect is a real symptom and byproduct of these disorders. This generation has the distinction of being the most obese, too.

Overeating and/or overindulging are other manifestations of perfection seeking, or avoidance of a felt sense of imperfection - or both. It can be a behavior to distract one from addressing their perception of a lack of achievement in their life, or suppressing the shame they may feel about their lot in life. As I say this, there are those who are fine with being overweight. Nothing says you must be a certain way. It really comes down to why we do what we do - and what the consequences are. Not everyone has the same reasons for engaging in the same behaviors. I'm not suggesting any of this is inherently bad or wrong. We can live our lives as we choose.

Do you want a good way to condition your child to learn that image is everything and that what you look like is critically important? How about a way to almost ensure they'll end up basing their self-esteem and worth on their appearance - and have them forever compare themselves to others? Enter them into a beauty pageant for kids! Heck, why not encourage them be a model, too? To me, there's not much more ridiculous and potentially damaging than seeing a five year old (like Jon-Benet Ramsey) all dolled up in a gown, with makeup and eyeliner, earrings and hair all done up, belting out a Broadway tune on stage for the judges. Like any other situation, there are exceptions and each kid is equipped differently to handle situations differently.

Quite frankly, I really don't have many opinions (mostly because I know they mean nothing in reality) but I do feel this is a good way to damage your kid and condition them to perceive and judge based on appearances first. We already live in a society where image is king, and where projecting the "right and perfect" image is valued. Why pile it on? It's already in our collective consciousness, so we don't need to hammer it home, do we? We don't need to increase the chances of our kid growing up one day obsessed with plastic surgery because they just can't accept the way they actually appear, do we?

This message and promise to deliver perfection has no boundaries. It's rampant in the self-help movement in the form of books, seminars, retreats, DVD's and dating sites that claim to have the perfect match just for you! There's nothing wrong with dating sites, but let's be honest. This message is all over the place, infusing (and infecting) our culture and collective consciousness in ways that feel overwhelming and virtually impossible to meet. The implications and its effects are devastating to say the least. Somehow we've come to believe that more is better and that acquiring more, better or different than the next guy is a recipe for getting us closer to the perfection we seek - just like the magazines promise.

Underlying this drive is an unspoken agreement that we're competing with each other, and our end result must be better than the next guy if we want to win. All the big corporations and all the competing interests, driven by the media and advertisers that fuel our economy, are making out like bandits pocketing huge sums of money. Apparently, that's of higher value, isn't it? The quality of our relationships and how we view ourselves has become secondary.

What we live we teach and pass on – to our children and grandchildren. Our overall sense of well being usually takes a backseat to the message that profit seeks. The end justifies the means - and sadly, it works. Until we wake up to what's going on and really see its impact, we can only create more of the same.

In our striving for this illusory state of perfection, at best, many of us become comfortably numb, outwardly content, yet inwardly unsatisfied. We end up living a life of quiet desperation, wondering how we ended up this way. It was never part of the plan, and we certainly never envisioned it this way. As a kid, we never said, "When I grow up, I want to be the kind of person who unconsciously chases after the illusion called 'perfection' in all phases of my life. I want to feel a need to project a certain image and worry about what others think of me. In the meantime, I want to spend massive amounts of time and energy suppressing and trying to accept my perceived imperfections, because it's much more difficult that way!"

Life just happens, doesn't it? The law of our experience also dictates that the more unconscious we are, the more we'll get what we don't want. Since it's not part of our make up, and since perfection doesn't actually exist in reality, how else *can* we feel when we chase after something that's unreal? Conversely, what we run from can only chase us. We're in a real dilemma where we run from many things - and chase after many things simultaneously.

Inner peace becomes a "nice idea for others" who aren't nearly as busy as we are. We tell ourselves we don't have the luxury or time for that, remaining mostly unaware of the true source of our existential discomfort. We just need the courage to face an altogether different direction - and then head in that direction, courageously. But first, we must be aware of the direction we're presently facing. We spend so much time looking in directions where problems present themselves, so inevitably we spend so much time and energy trying to solve our problems. We often label them as "confusing", "irritating" and even "depressing."

For some of us, our lives become a negotiation with solving one problem after the other, an endless job of problem management. We identify with this occupation and don't even know who we'd be without them. When we fill out the box that asks for our occupation on the IRS form, we write, "endless problem solver." Whether consciously or not, we label our problems "imperfect" - and certainly not "complete with all the requisite parts." Rarely do we consider that problems only exist in the mind - and not in reality.

Without referring to thought, do you have *any* problems? Without referring to the past, do you actually have a problem? No, you don't. Resist the urge to shrug off the utter simplicity of this direct recognition! Truth IS simple. Only thought tells you it's a problem. Put another way, in the absence of thought, is there an issue? No, there isn't. As Walt Whitman said, *"There is no imperfection in the present and none in the future."* We don't see that all of our problems are imaginary, and in fact, unreal. Situations in life are not problematic, regardless of how challenging. If we really look, situations are just that, situations and not problems.

Our so-called "problems" are created by the grasping and pushing away within the moment we begin to interpret, project, resist, compare, deny or judge a situation - transforming it from simple to complex. When we identify with this process - and take ownership, we stay mired in the very thing we *don't* want. Consciously, we tell ourselves we really don't want to experience this, and yet, unconsciously, we continue to feed this vicious cycle by negating what is.

Our ability to experience freedom from this downward cycle depends entirely on our capacity to notice the fact that we don't have real problems, only imagined ones! If we really want to be free from the tyranny of our mind, and the emotions that follow, we must be willing to see how it functions and what it does. We must be willing to consider (or just SEE) that we *have* a mind, and that we *aren't* our mind. If this is so, we inquire into why we keep identifying with the thoughts in our head? If we really want freedom, we must learn to embrace the heat of the fire, which we usually avoid at all costs.

We must be willing to experience the burning, the burning of pride, of arrogance, ignorance and limiting beliefs. We must embrace the burning of protecting ourselves from the unknown, what we fear and what we *think* we know. If we don't, we just get more of the same. If we don't, our freedom comes from the temporary moments where we've experienced something delightful, where we've read something from another that resonates deep within, or where we've temporarily witnessed breathtaking beauty in nature.

Granted, that's all nice as far as experience goes, but it's fleeting and doesn't remain. As with all experience, it must come and go, leaving you right where you were before - not knowing what's actual, and guaranteeing future angst. Our very freedom exists right in the middle of the heat of the fire and nowhere else, before and after experience. When we recognize that it is in the midst of that fire where our liberation lies, we allow ourselves to welcome the fire as our friend, something on our side - and not something to fear. We must allow ourselves to be consumed by that fire.

All we have to do is recognize what's going on in our minds. It takes no great intelligence at all; it just takes an earnest desire to see and observe with an impartial awareness what's happening, as it's happening. When we ask ourselves, "What's the payoff here?" When we ask, "Is this really for my highest good?" - and have the courage to answer honestly, do we begin to loosen the mind's hold on us. Only then can we begin to understand that we'll never be free as long as we cling to the endless ideas and beliefs in our minds. Only then do we allow for another potential to arise in our experience, one where we're no longer in opposition to reality, but in harmony with it.

When we clearly notice the grasping and avoiding nature of our minds, we begin to realize why we have this existential discomfort that feels like an itch in our minds. It's an itch we often conclude can only be alleviated by attaining what we think will satisfy us, or avoiding what we think won't. When we see that nothing has ever truly satisfied the longing in our minds, and that nothing *can* truly satisfy the longing in our minds, do we give ourselves a chance of experiencing reality directly, and not filtered through our ideas about it.

When we notice that it's never been about what the mind says it's about, we give ourselves an opportunity to see that there's nothing to get. Only then do we give ourselves a chance to see that what we're really after has no form – and that it can't be grasped, attained or achieved, do we play by the rules.

Like the scorpion's nature is to sting, we are wise to understand the nature of our situation; we recognize that the nature of the mind is to grasp and chase after what doesn't ultimately fulfill … and resists what it thinks wont' fulfill. Both movements only disturb, and never bring the formless peace, love and fulfillment we really want. This existential itch can only be rooted out when we notice these movements are inseparable from reality and the law of our experience. When we *see* these movements only hurt and divide, we can intend for something else, but certainly not before we *see*. Seeing that the mind is a master at labeling situations as good or bad, perfect or imperfect, and pleasant or unpleasant, we see that it only thinks in dualistic terms.

Seeing that situations are just that, and seeing that the mind labels them as good or bad, we see *how* we create our experience. When we identify with the mind, as the mind goes, we go. If we desire to be in harmony with life and ourselves, we notice that labels lie. We notice that whatever label we give something can't ever accurately describe that thing or situation. However, we notice how *it sets the mold and lays the foundation for how we experience* that thing or situation. If we label something "imperfect," inevitably, we won't be satisfied. If we view ourselves *in terms of* our perceived inadequacies, shortcomings and flaws, naturally we feel less than - and perhaps undeserving and deficient, won't we?

Labels lie and they lie all the time, especially when we see their ultimate use and function. The "problem" is we believe in them to be accurate representations for what they're describing. Instead of seeing aspects of ourselves (or situations we face) as the way it is - without any conceptual labels, positive or negative, we add an unnecessary layer on top in order to make sense of it. We mistakenly conclude that in order for us to understand something, we must label it. To label is to control. This is one of the many functions of our minds. The mind, in its lack of humility and ultimate ignorance, thinks it knows best and therefore, overshadows our being that really knows the deal.

While our being just watches on with impartial delight, even humor … and patiently waits for when it's called on, the mind continues unaware. The mind actually thinks that whatever conceptual model or label it comes up with is an actual and real substitute for reality - and this is never true. Although it may be very tempting to dismiss this observation, continuing to ignore its implications can have potentially devastating effects. Believing that our conceptions and interpretations are accurate representations for what's actually occurring, our knowledge becomes skewed and distorted.

Whether we realize it or not, feel it or not, disguise it or not, what we all want is truth. There's something within us that knows nothing less will satisfy. We erroneously look for it in concepts, belief systems and opinions – all creations manufactured and sustained in and by our minds. And yet it's never to late to *see* this. Resist the temptation to believe it takes time. It doesn't require a process or journey to see this. All processes and journeys imply time.

You can see this right now.

Chapter 4
Paradox & Confusion

"Have no fear of perfection – you'll never reach it."
~ Salvador Dali

"The dance of imperfection" doesn't involve doing any sidestepping movements, where we avoid or deny the challenges we face. As cool as it looks, it certainly doesn't involve shadow dancing, where we turn the lights out and watch our shadow (our particular challenge) dancing on the wall, forever beyond our reach. The "dance of imperfection" requires that we understand life is paradoxical. It invites us to see the inevitable confusion when we fail to recognize these paradoxes operating in our lives. Dancing with our perceived imperfections, face to face, we wholeheartedly embrace all that we are. In this way, suffering and/or confusion won't arise for us anymore.

In other words, we *dance,* elegantly and gracefully, with our unique and "less than ideal traits and abilities" that only we possess, knowing we are so much more than we appear to be. We dance with what we've been given, never apologizing or being ashamed of how we are - as we are. A paradox is understood to be an apparent contradiction, where two things appear to exclude each other - cancel each other out, but in reality don't. A practical example would be that in order to have a particular experience, one must not want to have that experience, or not strive to have that experience.

It reminds me of the quote from John of The Cross, *"In order to have everything, desire to have nothing."* Similarly, when you want to hold water in the palms of your hands, grasping won't do the job. If we remain open to the reality of paradoxes in our lives, we give ourselves the ability to see how they operate and unfold in our experience. We see that it is the nature of our human condition to be both saint *and* sinner - and not saint *or* sinner. It is this *both and* realization of our human nature (and not *either or)* that allows us to transcend the confusion that arises from misunderstanding.

Failure to understand this has created so much suffering and confusion in the past - and continuing to deny this can only create more suffering and confusion. Living in a world of duality and opposites, humanity is limited, and yet, this limitation doesn't define us. We are infinite Spirit at the same time. In truth, our infinite and *real* nature encompasses and includes our finite, limited nature. If this is the case, wisdom blooms when we include all of ourselves equally - not just the parts we like.

Essential to living a life of relative inner peace and contentment is our willingness to be honest with ourselves. Integrity and living a life that won't be looked back on in regret go hand in hand. We can't have one without the other. Essential to living a life of inner peace and contentment is our refusal to deceive ourselves. A common theme central in all spiritual traditions in history has been to "Know Thyself". In other words, if you only do one thing in life, make sure you know yourself. In order to know oneself, one must not engage in self-deception.

In order to know oneself, one must be willing to see what's true, no matter what. If we are earnest in our desire to see through the false, it's much easier to tell the truth. Honesty with the self, about the self, is essential if we are to enjoy our lives so that we won't have regrets on our deathbed, wishing we could do it over. Life isn't a dress rehearsal - this is it. A mind that is being watched tends to become more humble. With greater awareness comes a greater capacity to live from what we know is true - not we suspect or believe is true.

Humility has a way of showing us our preoccupation with our illusions. Humility is like having an extra guard on duty, flagging us when our pride is preventing us from telling the truth. Having a good amount of humility is requisite if we are to be honest with who we are, *as* we are. It allows us to see ourselves not in some enhanced, made-up light, but rather, under the bright lights, naked with warts and all. Real humility allows us the capacity to laugh at ourselves and not take ourselves so seriously. Real humility equips us to be less a victim of the mind, and more its master.

Otherwise, we are just wound tight, aren't we? And more inclined to bring about (quite possibly the most damaging kind of dishonesty there is) ... denial of our mixed human nature, the reality of our "both and" make up. Refusing to acknowledge all of our unique strengths, abilities and character traits - and all of our *not so great* traits and characteristics speaks to our fears in facing what we deem "flawed" or "imperfect." What do we imagine will happen if we admit the whole truth to ourselves? Who would we be then? Could we live with ourselves, and if we could, where might this integrity lead?

Clinging to an unquestioned belief that we must hide aspects of ourselves, aspects that we're either ashamed of or embarrassed by, further solidifies our faulty interpretation. We fail to see that we're all in the very same boat, sailing along through the journey of life with very similar struggles simply disguised differently. We fail to see that most of us have demons inside - but with a different voice and face. By the wayside goes the realization that in our mutually shared acknowledgment of *all* that we are, real healing happens ... the kind that liberates. The Saints and Sages that we honor to this day we honor for a reason: they were willing to be honest with themselves about their dual nature, their *both and* nature.

They knew that the "either or" perception was illusory and didn't exist, and was the thing that brought about suffering. Being ignorant to what's true, we must suffer. These people did what Walt Whitman once said, "dismiss whatever insults your soul" ... without denying any aspect of themselves. They knew that in our brokenness, we are made whole, and that wholeness doesn't exclude those parts that are less desirable.

We can hear the words of the Sufi poet, Rumi in his poem titled, "Undressing."

Learn the alchemy true beings know.
The moment you accept what troubles

you've been given; the door will be open.
Welcome difficulty, as a familiar comrade.
Joke with torment brought by the friend.

Sorrows are the rags of old clothes
and jackets that serve to cover,
and then are taken off.

That undressing,
and the naked body underneath,
is the sweetness that comes after grief.

In my second book, *"When Wisdom Blooms – Awaken the Sage Within"* ... I noted that dogs and cats have no concept of perfection and imperfection. They have no idea that what is presently happening shouldn't be happening - or that it could be happening in any other way. As a result, they don't suffer psychologically or emotionally. They are as they are, without any inkling of improving, or the desire to make their circumstances better.

Dogs and cats are perfect as they are, just like nature. Like animals, nature doesn't tell stories, either. Nature expresses itself as it is, freely unencumbered, without any regret or longing. Granted, animals and nature don't have discriminating minds, but that's the point. The fact that we do reveals that it's our minds that tell us there's a problem! But here's the thing we can notice:

The fact that we possess a discriminating mind doesn't exclude us from being perfect just the way we are!

What's wrong with absolutely anything unless you think about it? What's wrong with right now unless you think about it? Again, resist the urge to dismiss this powerful pointer that can reveal the truth. Resist the temptation to habitually latch on to a conclusion that says something like, "It's a ridiculous notion to even entertain such a statement, and a notion that will only lead me to the land of resignation, where I'll be walked on like a doormat!" I hope that you don't infer this, only because this grossly unexamined inference is absolutely illusory and untrue. Don't believe me. Find out for yourself.

If we are to find a real and solid manifestation of perfection *anywhere in reality*, we can always look to nature. An elegant swan cleaning its mate as they float in a lake, and a cherry blossom tree in full bloom suggests perfection. A beautiful sunset displaying various colors at the opportune moment - and a vivid rainbow after a sudden and passing summer thundershower suggests perfection. The sound of the wind caressing the leaves in the autumn trees on a crisp, October day, and a pod of whales singing as they swim by a tour boat in Hawaii suggests perfection. While they aren't actually two, nature and perfection are wedded, like the bird in the sky, or like the infant breastfeeding in its mother's arms.

Like the constant ebb and flow of the tides in continuous display and in enjoyment of itself, everything unfolds perfectly. Nature doesn't have to *try* to enjoy itself as it expresses; it just does, naturally.

Hear the words of Emerson as he said, *"These roses under my window make no reference to former roses or better ones; they are for what they are; they exist with God today. There is no time for them. There is simply the rose and it is perfect in every moment of its existence. But man postpones or remembers; he does not live in the present, but with reverted eye laments the past, or heedless of the riches that surround him, stands on tiptoe to foresee the future. He cannot be happy and strong until he, too, lives with Nature in the present, above time."*

When humans *try* to enjoy themselves, they almost always have a difficult time. It's a wonderful paradox, actually - and one that frequently leaves us feeling frustrated and confused. We might say, "I really don't understand it; I made all the necessary preparations and made sure all the conditions were just right. I tried to make you happy, and it was a complete failure!" We forget that in order to really enjoy something, we must allow for it to happen, naturally and spontaneously. The more absent we are, the more present we are - and enjoyment just happens.

When we're clearly addicted to something, say a chemical substance that's creating so much pain in our lives, we can only begin the road to recovery when we surrender - when we give in. Only when we acknowledge that we are slaves to that chemical do we give ourselves a real chance at abstaining from that chemical. Recognizing *and then accepting* our powerlessness over the situation, we render ourselves powerful and able to respond appropriately. Response - ability. Whenever we don't understand the paradox of a particular situation we're faced with, odds are we will continue to approach (or relate *to)* that situation in a way that will further ensure us being in bondage to it.

Instead of not making any demands on the moment, we have a tendency to believe we need to "add to or subtract from" the moment in the hope of having a "better" or more complete experience - or at least, one that's more in harmony with what we *think* we want. I say, "think" because isn't it true that often what we think we want, (upon further examination) isn't what we really want? Paradoxically, when we give up trying to alter or change the moment - or when we give up thinking we must have something in a particular way, enjoyment arises and confusion eventually disappears.

As a result, we often discover that what we really want shows up. When we clearly recognize that all of our striving for perfection is really about our desire to feel whole and complete, we allow for new possibilities to arise in our experience. When we see what's true, something lets go, and we're no longer bound. Until we break free of the unconscious, trance-like mode we've been operating from, we'll never experience our true desire - to *experientially feel* that completeness, where nothing needs to be added to or subtracted from. This is perfection.

The perception of this wholeness and completeness, whether we realize it, is what we're really after - and nothing less will satisfy. Since no label or description can capture reality, we suffer when we mistakenly label aspects of ourselves as "imperfect and flawed" - as opposed to seeing that these aspects of ourselves are "as they are." When this happens, we inevitably experience the fractured hurt and dis-ease that comes with labels that always lie. Like Winnie the Pooh stuck in the rabbit hole, man is forever stuck and identified with his lack of awareness and knowledge of himself, *until* he is willing to look beyond apparent causes to the real source within.

It's all so simple really, but our minds insist on complicating things, until it doesn't anymore. All we need to do is want a different possibility, and be willing to examine our direct experience, consciously tracing it back to the perception that led us astray. Then and only then, are we able to take a different path, a path that isn't divisive. Seeing clearly the nature and reality of our situation, we are aware that we live in a world that isn't perfectible; we're aware that we live in a world that often displays a *sense* of incompleteness, a *sense* that something is fractured and unfinished.

Arising from this sense of discomfort is a sense of being wounded, with the feeling we won't ever heal. Having difficulty imagining future happiness, we believe our situation is permanent, pervasive and personal. Instead of looking to heal something that we aren't even quite sure is actually wounded in the first place, we can look beyond *the appearance of imperfection and inadequacy* - and look to the wisdom of insecurity. In a world where absolutely nothing lasts, where nothing remains, we see that we can't cling to anything at all - including our very life - *and* feel remotely comforted. Without pushing away the reality of the situation we find ourselves in, we give ourselves permission - we give ourselves license - to simply allow whatever's arising to be just the way it is; we know that it's all perfect and complete already.

And if we really look closely, we recognize that none of it is personal at all. If we don't yet see it, we look until we *do* see. Our comfort resides in true perception, not pursuing some state of perfection we think will comfort us. Working with the law of nature and our experience (same thing) we see the wisdom of *transcending and including all of it,* for we know that to resist any part of it is unintelligent and nonsensical.

Consciousness has a habitual tendency to forget that it is our orientation *towards* our struggles and challenges that creates the problems. We project onto others own feelings of inner frustration and disappointment - and we don't take responsibility for our experience.

We forget it's ALL an inside game, always and in all ways. In addition, our culture has a tendency to operate from the notion that the way to effect real psychological and emotional healing is to cover over the wound with temporary, band-aid approaches. We spend our efforts and energy on correcting the *effects* instead of the *causes* - through justification, rationalization, minimizing and a variety of other distracting methods. Whether our end goal is the pursuit of happiness, or the avoidance of pain, the destination is a shared one. That destination is an unfulfilled place where existential discomfort resides because we don't recognize the nature of the paradoxes we find ourselves in. We don't see that the cure for pain is *in* the pain.

We don't yet see that *what we run from can only chase us, and what we pursue can only evade us.* Try to make something perfect and it will forever remain imperfect. Try to have fun - and fun evades you. Nature is effortlessly perfect, and effort is perfectly imperfect. When it comes to how we see ourselves, effort presupposes we must do something to fix or change the way we are. Reality (and our un-blemished true nature) is always right here, before labels and descriptions - immediate, undivided and already complete.

When we believe our labels and descriptions can capture reality, we often experience contraction. Paradoxically, when we resist the urge to label and describe, we innocently meet the moment as it is and not as we wish. And there's no contraction.

When I was twenty years old, I had the good fortune of going on a family cruise to Bermuda to celebrate my parent's 25th anniversary. Riding a moped alone one day, I noticed a path in the bush on the side of the road that led to an opening with a view of the ocean. I felt compelled to pull over, park the moped and wonder over to the path. I continued to walk about two hundred feet until I found myself at the edge, where the island met the ocean. I sat down and began gazing out into the vast, clearest aqua-blue water I had ever seen.

I don't know how long I sat there, perhaps twenty minutes or so, but I was lost in the view, not sensing any boundary between what I was seeing and what was doing the seeing. There was just absolute and total peace in that still silence - and a feeling of being both totally absent and totally present at the same time.

I was taken back, never imagining I could have such a wonderful and compete experience like this. After a while, I remember saying to myself, "this is so beautiful and I don't want it to ever end." And it was in that exact moment (when I became aware of myself sitting there enjoying and being immersed in the view) that the experience ended. Instantly jolted, I was transported back in identification with a mind that was looking out at the scene. In my desire to hold onto the experience and make it last longer, it ceased. It was the first time in my life that I noticed that self-consciousness terminated the experience.

This reminds me of a famous Zen story we can all relate to:

A Zen master was making a painting and he had his main student sit by his side to tell him when his painting was perfect. The master was worried and the student was also worried because he had never seen his teacher do anything imperfect. However, that day things started going awry. The master tried and the more he tried, the more it was a mess. In Japan or China, the art of calligraphy is done on rice paper, on a certain paper, a very sensitive and fragile paper. If you hesitate just a little, for centuries it can be known where the calligrapher hesitated, because more ink spreads into the rice paper, making it a mess.

It is very difficult to deceive on rice paper and the master knew it. You have to go on flowing; you are not to hesitate, even for a single moment. If you hesitate for a split second, what to do? You already missed, and one who has a keen eye will immediately say, "It is not a Zen painting at all" because a Zen painting has to be a spontaneous and free flowing painting. The master tried and tried and the more he tried, the more he perspired. The student was sitting there and shaking his head back and forth saying, "No, this isn't perfect." Consequently, the master made more mistakes.

Then the ink began to run out so the master said, "You go out and prepare more ink." While the student was outside preparing the ink, the master did his masterpiece. When the student came in he said, "Master, but this is perfect, what happened?" The master laughed and said, "I became aware of one thing, your presence. The very idea that someone was there to appreciate or condemn, to say yes or no, disturbed my inner tranquility. Now I will never be disturbed. I have come to know that I was trying to make it perfect and that was the only reason for it not being perfect."

Try to make something perfect and it won't ever be. Being self-conscious and exerting a lot of effort in the hopes of making something just right only distorts. Do it naturally and it is always perfect. Nature is perfect and effort and striving isn't. True seeing sees the perfection in all things, as they are. Wisdom sees the inherent beauty and completeness in everything God has made. It is the evaluating, comparing mind that labels things imperfect and flawed. Whichever you identify yourself with determines what you see, and therefore, what you experience.

Conventional wisdom would try to tell us that if perfection is an actual and attainable state, then imperfection, too, must be an actual state that can be avoided or removed. This "wisdom" implies if we are to accept and embrace those aspects of ourselves (that we don't particularly like or appreciate) that those aspects will become more apparent in our daily experience.

In other words, we think they'll have more of an influence in our daily lives if we don't suppress, run from or resist them. Conventional wisdom and conditioning would try to tell us that the way to deal with pain (or that which we don't like) is to deny its existence - or at the least resist its presence in our experience. That way, it reasons, its life span will be short and the impact minimal. It then infers that embracing and welcoming is for passive wimps, for those who don't get up and "fight" for what they want. In truth, "Blessed are the meek, for they shall inherit the earth."

Since this kind of "wisdom" comes from the mind that resists what is, and not from the heart that already knows, it's no wonder things go awry. While we continue to identify with the mind and its distorted view, we won't ever escape the byproducts of those views. The antidote and the restoration of true perception lies in understanding the paradoxes we continually find ourselves in. The antidote is to accept and embrace these paradoxes so *that we don't continue to give life to* the kinds of experiences we'd prefer not to have.

A fitting poem by *Rumi*:

Silkworms

The hurt you embrace
Becomes joy.

Call it to your arms
Where it can change.

A silkworm eating leaves
Makes a cocoon.

Each of us weaves a chamber
Of leaves and sticks.

Silkworms begin to truly exist
As they disappear inside that room.

Without legs, we fly.
When I stop speaking,

This poem will close,
And open its silent wings …

If we want to remember something that we're temporarily forgetting, we don't want to stress and strain and search our mind for the answer, right? We all know that the answer comes when we let go of needing to know in that moment. If aware, we say, "Oh, I will remember it later if I stop thinking about it." Sure enough, the answer pops up later when we aren't thinking about it. If we are meditating (or sitting in silence as I prefer to call it) for the purpose of rest or relaxation and find our mind racing, don't resist this movement of thinking. We can't relax by forcing relaxation, can we? Rather, we just let the thoughts go by like clouds in the vast, empty sky, watching our mind - and let the quiet stillness reveal itself.

If we want something gone from our experience, it *only* dissolves when we let it be there in the first place. Offer it no resistance and watch it leave. If we lean towards being the lazy kind (and would rather be more productive) fully allow yourself to be the lazy kind until something else moves you. If you don't worry about how to know when to move, you'll know when to move - but *only* if you welcome laziness to be present.

If we want that baby crying on the airplane to stop driving us nuts, we stop telling ourselves the baby shouldn't be crying - and watch the annoyance diminish or go away. Don't let your interpretations and conclusions *about* concepts become so real that you mistake them for *being* the reality - and not just symbols for the reality. Don't confuse the symbols and the things they aim to represent; don't marry the two, as they are forever meant to be divorced. Indeed, the "map is not the territory" and the map can only describe a territory in such a way as to help us traverse that territory, not to mistake them as being the same. Granted, it's a useful tool but our perception of the map can never equal the territory.

If you have a real challenge accepting your perceived limitations or "imperfections" in your life - and they're renting a whole lot of space in your head, then stop believing the thoughts in your head that tell you that you should be different than you are. If we want someone we really care about to "change their ways" or "see the light" ... see that it's more about our need for them to be different than they are. When we offer no resistance and judgment to them as they are, over time, watch what happens to them.

One of the greatest gifts you can give another is *your* higher consciousness and unconditional acceptance, the kind that dispels ignorance. Work with yourself, not against yourself. By working with yourself, you effectively work with others. You are the ultimate and final authority in your experience - and what you live, you teach. But hey, don't believe me.

In closing, a verse from **The Tao Te Ching:**

To be whole, let yourself break.
To be straight, let yourself bend.
To be full, let yourself be empty.
To be new, let yourself wear out.
To have everything, give everything up.
Knowing others is a kind of knowledge;

Knowing yourself is wisdom
Conquering others requires strength;
Conquering yourself is true power.
To realize you have enough is true wealth.
Pushing ahead may succeed,
But staying put brings endurance.
Die without perishing and find the eternal.
To know that you do not know is strength.
Not knowing that you do not know is a sickness.
The cure begins with the recognition of the sickness.
Knowing what is permanent: enlightenment
Not knowing what is permanent: disaster.
Knowing what is permanent opens the mind.
Open mind, open heart.
Open heart, magnanimity.

Chapter 5
Beyond Seeming Opposites

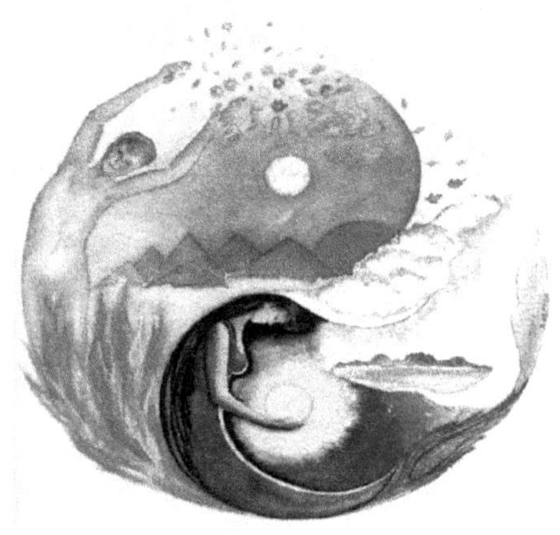

"Now the two primal Spirits, who reveal themselves in vision as Twins, are the Better and the Bad, in thought and word and action. Between these two the wise ones chose aright; the foolish not so."

~ *Zoroaster*

Man's ongoing dilemma has been mis-identifying his own intellectual conclusions as reality. These inherently limited assumptions and suppositions are the end result of an arbitrary point of perception based on (and a direct consequence of) his past conditioning and habitual patterns of thinking. We see what we believe and believe what we see … and then we often wonder how we create our experience. Understanding comes from operating from the appropriate context, asking the right questions and looking in the direction where the "answer" or truth can reveal itself. Sometimes, there isn't an answer - and that's acceptable for the one who doesn't need to know. It's acceptable for the one who knows that in order for truth to be revealed, one must be willing *not* to know.

If, on the other hand, we are to declare something as true or real based upon hasty and simple examination, we invariably end up with a distorted conclusion that hurts. Our conclusions don't mean much if, as a result of those conclusions, we end up feeling confused, alienated and incomplete. Our conclusions don't mean much unless we're willing to take the next step and question if they're actually true. Otherwise, we forever remain feeling isolated from the completeness and wholeness of Life and live from a fiction of our own making. Life isn't divided. Man's perception is divisive. Consequently, in a world without division, man divides.

Until man sees that there are no causes in the observable world - and that the world he sees and observes is the world of effects, not much will change for him. Unlike any other species, humans have developed language as its primary means of communication, both spoken and written. We all know that it takes years to learn the various labels for existence and eventually string them together into a story that makes sense. Babies have no idea what words mean right out of the womb.

Words have no intrinsic meaning. They're just sounds and symbols that point to life's happenings. The words "happiness" and "joy" mean absolutely nothing to the aborigine in Australia. By nature, language is both dualistic and divisive, and sends us on all kinds of wild goose chases. Let me rephrase that: It is our translation *of* language that sends us on all kinds of wild goose chases - and not language itself.

If I classify something based on its appearance and function, then things that don't appear and function just like it are said to be something other, or "not" that - and classified as something else. I draw the line between *this* thing and *those* things that aren't just like it. If this tall thing with leaves that grows out of the ground is different in appearance than anything else, I might call it a "tree." Anything that doesn't appear and function like a tree is not that (a tree) - and I might call it something else, like a "rock" or a "bird" or a "mountain." There's the parasite and the host; there's the infection and the cure; there's addiction and recovery, and there's Hitler and Mother Theresa.

Like life, we can never quite pin down language; it is forever in flux and never carved in stone. The Greek philosopher Heraclitus said, "We can never step in the same river twice." Due to the constant flux and flow, new water is always rushing by, never being the same water. We speak of language as if it is something fixed and true - and something that we can rely on to tell us what's so. However, believing we always perceive language correctly is like thinking we can step in the same river twice.

We use, hear or read the same concept numerous times, but *we seldom seem to question why it is that the meaning tends to change over time.* Doesn't its meaning alter depending on our understanding and level of awareness? Doesn't its meaning change depending on who the perceiver is?

For instance, aren't there occasions when your interpretation of a profound insight or passage is different from when you were previously exposed to it? Of course it is. Doesn't this speak to its ultimate (and relative) accuracy and true function? In other words, the one who perceives is the one who draws their own meaning; the interpretation changes relative to where that perceiver is in terms of their level of awareness. This being the case, wouldn't this pertain to how we see ourselves, too? If one day we have a difficult time accepting a certain personal characteristic, but the next day we could care less, what does that tell you? That just maybe we make it all up?

Additionally, implicit in language is the notion that concepts are *either or* and not *both and.* Being wired to avoid pain and gain pleasure, humans naturally resist the "bad or unpleasant side" of the conceptual symbol called *joy,* of the conceptual symbol called *comfort* and of the conceptual symbol called *life.* Pushing away the certain realities of their opposites - pain, discomfort and eventual death - is a reliably effective formula for continued angst and anxiety! Please check it out for yourself; you are the final authority! Until we see that *any* movement we make is a movement away, and of resistance, we are destined to function like washing machines stuck on the "repeat" cycle.

In our abiding trance-like state of misunderstanding the true purpose and function of language, we unwittingly invite unpleasant experiences. We thank God for all the "good" and pleasant things that come our way, calling them "blessings" - and yet we don't ever consider thanking Him for the "bad" and unpleasant things that happen to us. And this is exactly where we go astray. Incidentally, this is also where the New Age Movement goes astray.

Have you ever really pondered why life comes in opposites? Why everything you deem worthy and of value is one of a pair of opposites? Why each decision you make is between opposites - and every desire you have is based in polar opposites? We see how spatial dimensions are opposing - up versus down, left versus right, long versus short, inside versus outside, here versus there and top versus bottom. We notice the things that have greater importance to us personally come in opposites as well: pleasure versus pain, good versus evil, comfort versus discomfort, acceptance versus resistance, freedom versus enslavement, God versus Satan, Heaven versus Hell, truth versus falsehood and life versus death.

The more subjective "eye of the beholder" qualities come in opposites, too: beautiful versus ugly, smart versus dumb, strong versus weak, success versus failure, and dare I seemingly contradict the central theme of this entire book and say, perfect versus imperfect? Every time we make a decision, we draw a boundary line between our options to choose from. When we desire something, we draw a boundary line between the pleasurable thing we desire and the unpleasant thing we don't want - and then move towards the thing we do want.

To sustain a particular belief means we draw a dividing boundary line between what we believe to be true and what we don't believe is true. To sustain a particular energetic feeling sense of insecurity over some aspect of ourselves, we draw a boundary line between secure and insecure. Thus, we tell ourselves we won't ever feel secure until we improve upon, fix or change our weakness. All of these dividing lines are not boundaries at all. In fact, the boundaries we perceive are entirely MENTAL - and have no more existence in reality than Snow White and the Seven Dwarves!

If peace and self-acceptance is what we're after, we don't have the luxury of pitting one side against the other side. We don't have the luxury in believing in - or stopping at - the appearance of things. We must go beyond the appearance and look to the essence *behind* the appearance. On closer examination, we notice that delineating a boundary line doesn't distinguish anything but an inside versus an outside. Imagine a circle you've just drawn on a piece of paper. Better yet, please take out a piece of paper and do this now. And in that circle, you've written the word "inside." Right next to the circle, on a blank sheet of paper, you've written the word "outside." Notice that the opposites of "inside versus outside" didn't exist until you drew the boundary of the circle. That is, the boundary line created the pair of opposites, did it not?

Simply put, to draw a boundary line means to create and maintain opposites. To draw a boundary line means to distinguish this from that - and then we believe "this" and "that" are forever set apart. With this recognition, we can begin to recognize we live in a world of opposites because our lives are spent drawing and believing in opposites! We live in a world of opposites that create conflict and suffering. Where we decide to draw the line is precisely where the war takes place. The more entrenched that battle line is drawn, the more bloody that war becomes. The same thing that gives you pleasure gives you pain. The more that pleasure is absent, the more that discomfort is present. The more I try to maintain pleasurable states, the more I fear uncomfortable states.

Having a death grip on a need to be successful, the more I naturally fear failure. The more I steadfastly cling to life, the more frightened I am of my inevitable death. The more I strive for happiness, the deeper my sadness has a tendency to get. The more I pursue trying to project my most perfect self, the more obsessed I become with hiding what I'm insecure about. The more I am concerned with how others view me, the more insecure I feel - and the more I try to hide those aspects of myself I deem less worthy. To the degree that I value anything at all, to that degree do I become obsessed with its loss, and so on.

This orientation only ensures that I live my life in a contrived manner, attempting to manufacture and sustain some ideal image I've cooked up for myself - and hope it lasts as long as possible. Since it never matches up with reality, it can't last - and I must suffer the consequences. Illusion hurts, and the division we create is the wood-chipper we walk right into, tearing us apart. No longer am I in harmony with life because I've placed a conceptual barrier between my experience and whatever arises. In other words, my problems are with the boundaries I create and believe in, and the opposites they *must* create. In so doing, I remove myself from the flow of life - and I feel that removal in my thoughts, emotions and experience.

And the cycle continues - until what's feeding the cycle is exposed and seen through. Believing the boundaries to be real - after all, everyone else does - we never seem to inquire into its actual reality. More specifically, believing our *mental* boundaries to be real, we assume the opposites are forever separate and divorced from each other - as if they are pitted *against* each other. Coming from this place, we imagine that our lives would be more peaceful and enjoyable if we could just get rid of the negative and undesired halves of the opposites! We'd be in heaven, here on earth, and have no problems. If we could just get rid of all of our unhappiness, restlessness, insecurity, sickness, spiritual and financial poverty, how great life would be!

In our imaginings, we don't recognize that "Heaven" isn't just the "good" aspect of the halves, but the transcendence of both halves - and "Hell" is a conglomeration and abundance of the "bad" half of the pairs of opposites. If history is indeed a great teacher, why don't we learn that centuries of avoiding and pushing away the undesired half (and clinging to the desired half) has NEVER been an effective formula for genuine and lasting happiness?

Despite all of our remarkable progress and advancements in medicine and technology, it's pretty evident that our culture is more anxious and discontented than ever. Our unconscious and habitual way of seeking happiness is to somehow get rid of one of the opposites - and it never works. There's nothing inherently wrong with progress or improvement, unless we depend on it for our satisfaction and ultimate contentment.

Believing that the goal of our experience is to only attract what we desire invites further anxiety and dis-ease. Not only does it go against the nature of how our experience works, it implies that the opposite formula, avoidance of the undesired half, is also wise. In the guise of taking "full responsibility" for our lives, we think we're being irresponsible if we allow the "bad" half to stick around in our experience. Ironically, it is this resistance to the undesired half that makes it stick around. Thus, we don't see the forest for the trees. Believing we create and attract our physical diseases is harming, causing a wide variety of feelings like anxiety, guilt, shame and despondency.

Having the notion that God is a partial and biased deity (that rewards and punishes us for our self-centered tendencies) only strengthens our belief that moving away from what we deem "bad or wrong" is a useful strategy. Our bodies are equipped with five sensing instruments that tell us whether we're in harmony with the "outside" world, but somehow we underestimate its value, and instead, defer to the mind to tell us what's so. Once we defer to the mind to tell us what's so, we get a whole new set of sensations to experience - and they're usually not in sync with reality, either!

Isn't it peculiar that we have a natural inclination to place a higher value on believing the thoughts and conclusions in our heads more than the instant feedback we get from our bodies, moment to moment?

Minds think dualistically; there's no debating this. All concepts are inherently dualistic. Because minds think conceptually, mind can't help *but* think dualistically. It believes it's either this or it's that. When we want this, we don't want that. When we embrace this, we must inevitably resist that. When we resist that, we must experience a certain amount of discomfort - *from that.* Wisdom sees that the nature of absolutely everything in the manifest world is "both and" ... not "either or"... so we are wise to not only include both, but welcome both – but only if we don't want to suffer! Your lover's sensitivity is both a liability and a gift. Your need to make things "just right" is both draining and admirable. The whining, two-year little boy or girl is both adorable and a pain in the butt most times, are they not?

On closer inspection, we notice something we may not have seen before. While it *appears* that experience seems to arise alone, the opposite experience (although much more subtle) also arises. In other words, every experience arises in dualism, and in unison. We recognize that there isn't any separation between the opposite experiences, regardless of what our mind tells us. Thinking conceptually, we see that dualistically is the *only* way the mind *can* see experience – "this" way or "that" way, the "good" way or the "bad" way, the "right" way or the "wrong" way.

However, when I want to experience rest and quiet, at the same time, I don't want to experience unrest and noise. When I like or prefer quietness, at the same time, I don't want to hear noise, at least not to the extent that might compromise the quietness I seek. When I prefer to enjoy quietness, my mind simultaneously dislikes noise. They arise *together*; mind can't see this, but YOU can. While one half is very obvious and easy to feel, the other is very subtle and difficult to feel, but they still arise together, at the same time. When I want to be alone, arising in that wanting to be alone is also the desire not to have company. When I insist on performing a particular task to my idea of perfection, also arising is my need to avoid actions and results that I deem "imperfect." When I fail to notice that this is how experience must unfold, I suffer to a certain degree.

My peace and security comes from *seeing* the necessity of both halves arising simultaneously, in order for experience to happen at all. Seeing this, gratitude naturally seeps in, even for the undesired half. Wisdom blooms when I recognize that this interplay and ongoing dance in nature is not only a functional necessity, but apparently possesses a check and balance system. If *this* arises, then *that*, too, must arise simultaneously. Wisdom blooms when I dance in harmony with that system, without needing to add or subtract anything. In an engaged yet detached manner, I don't identify with either arising. I rest in Spirit, that which gives rise to both - and I am free in this timeless moment. In this resting, all is balanced. In this resting, I notice balance is the reality.

With life comes death. In fact, without death, there could be no life. Human birth is the birth of opposites, of man and woman. The beating of our hearts as they open and close, pumping blood throughout our bodies and brains - and the muscles in our lungs that breathe in and out, are both necessary and vital movements operating in perfect harmony in order to for us to live and function.

Similarly, we look up and then we may look down; we turn right and we may turn left; we laugh and then we cry. We feel sad only to later feel happy; we love and we hate. The point is that *if* we have the option to do one thing, we must have the option to do the opposite thing.

This is how our world operates and this interplay is what informs our minds, letting us know what our options are. The entire world is a direct manifestation of these opposites, and in fact, couldn't exist if it not were for these pairs operating in unison all the time. Life is an intimate interaction and adventure of opposites - a dance if you will - where day turns into night and night turns into day. It's an amazing and ongoing dynamic, where the light shines and reveals everything, only to later have the darkness descend and hide everything.

High tide rolls in, hiding the rocky jetty that separates the beach from the adjacent one. Six hours later it recedes to low tide, revealing clams, starfish and seashells down by the waterline. This waterline appears to be a boundary - a dividing line between the beach and the ocean. However, the lines that appear to be dividing lines are precisely where the ocean and land touch each other. These lines *both* join *and* unite just as much as they divide and distinguish. Lines and boundaries are not the same thing; these lines are not boundaries! These "dividing lines" equally represent the place where the ocean and land meet.

It is indeed this constant ebb and flow that "makes the world go round" - and it is our understanding and orientation *to* this flow that determines the quality of our experience. If we fail to recognize and fully embrace that we can't have one experience without the other, and that we can't have this particular strength without its opposing weakness, we resist our experience. This resistance comes in the form of running toward or away from the moment, vacillating between pleasant and unpleasant emotions.

If we fail to see that in order to have our own unique set of strengths, skills and abilities that only we have, we won't see that we must also have our own unique set of weaknesses and "less than ideal" abilities, too. Consequently, we just may discover gratitude arising for all of it, as it is.

If we do see this, we can better understand and appreciate who we are, AS we are. How might your perception of your "imperfections" be different as a result? Would you have a different experience? Would it be possible that, as a result of seeing what's real, that believing in the existence of "imperfection" might drop away? You bet! If you think that this is just a sleight of hand, waving-away strategy that aims to soften and placate, think again. If you think this is just a matter of semantics, think again. If our strengths can't ever be "perfect," how can we ever rightly call our weaknesses, "imperfect?"

Jesus was one of the few teachers in all of the religious traditions that claimed to be both human *and* divine. Knowing he lived in a relative world of duality, Jesus didn't look to avoid any human experience. In fact, he saw the kingdom of heaven as right here, right now - right in the midst of any and all experience. Although perceived to be the Son of God, he definitely had his moments where his humanity came through. Some examples of his humanity were when, in a rage, he overturned the moneychanger's table, and as he was nailed to the cross he yelled out, *"My God, my God, why have you forsaken me?"*

In his moments of distress, Jesus couldn't help but express his human side, simultaneously possessing the capacity and consciousness to ultimately transcend his circumstance. His life was a living example of one who didn't adhere to the mind's collective insistence in the popular distinctions of "good" and "bad" ... "perfect" and "imperfect." His life was a clear example of one who lived beyond the mind-body experience, making such statements as, *"I am in the world, but not of it."* Looking beyond appearance to the essence, Jesus didn't use labels that lie. He knew better. He knew "the way" to awaken and be one with God was to see that the true nature of things wasn't "this or that" - or "black or white." He conveyed this by saying such things like, *"Blessed are the meek, for they shall inherit the earth"* and to the unbelieving Jews that saw only their limited nature, *"Ye are Gods, I tell you."*

His undistorted vision was rooted in something far beyond what the mind could ever understand and comprehend - and certainly beyond what the collective consciousness believed in at the time. When he said, *"I am in the world, but not of it"* we realize that Jesus saw that the way to be freed from the pairs of opposites, one had to have the direct and immediate realization that Spirit is NOT good versus evil, or pleasure versus pain, or life versus death. Jesus knew that Spirit is that which gives rise to the opposites ... impartially and with equanimity.

Therefore, Spirit is not the "good half" of the opposites, but the ground of all the opposites. Our "salvation" then, lies not in identifying with or chasing after the pleasant side of dualism, but to rest in the Source of both sides of duality, for that is what we are.

"Let this consciousness be in you that was in Christ Jesus." "I the Lord make the Light to fall on the good and the bad alike – I the Lord, do all these things." As a result of his true perception, he knew his oneness with God – and since he knew he was *both* human *and* divine, he made no distinctions and judgments about himself.

Since he didn't judge himself, he didn't judge others. Each person he encountered was perfect, whole and complete - no less or greater than he, including the man sentenced to death by stoning for his sins, and the prostitute shunned by the locals. He made statements like, *"Greater things than I will you do" … and "Let he who is without sin cast the first stone."* Sadly, Jesus' open teachings were considered a threat to the people of his time and he paid a huge price for sharing what he realized.

While we don't usually recognize this, in our constant judging and evaluating things as good or bad, right or wrong and pleasant or unpleasant, we essentially separate our selves from what's actually happening. In the form of concepts, assumptions, beliefs, judgments and opinions, we erect a seemingly solid wall of separation between our self and what's actually occurring. No longer are we intimately engaged in the moment, experiencing it as it is. Instead, we experience life's moments through the filter of our mind that's always describing what's happening in relation to its familiar and preferred story. In our ignorance, we divide and fracture. As Neale Donald Walsh accurately noted in Conversations With God, *"In the absence of that which is not, that which is, is not."*

My brain contracted in confusion when I first read that statement almost 15 years ago, but I noticed something else arise within that confusion. There was a sense of knowing expansion, albeit a small one - and that's what I ran with. It's made all the difference, and a huge one at that. I never thought I'd live one day welcoming the "negative and undesired stuff" in my experience. Paradoxically, seeing how it all works, you notice the negative stuff hardly arises anymore. Thought and the mind can never comprehend this - but YOU can. What is presently arising can't be any other way than it is.

Wisdom already sees this as clear as day, but the masses believe it is lunacy. Mark Twain said it best, *"When you find yourself in the majority, it's time to pause and reflect."* Wisdom knows that when we battle anything, we lose.

The wisdom of no escape invites us to see that we can't ever escape the way in which we interpret anything. It comes with the package, like the west wind down the New Jersey Shore brings greenhead flies that bite. We can easily confirm this for ourselves. Simply put, it goes like this: We interpret the moment based on our beliefs and conditioning; we feel or experience that interpretation in our bodies, in the form of uncomfortable emotions like contraction, anxiety, depression and dis-ease, or to the more enjoyable and preferred comfortable emotions and sensations like openness, lightness, resonance, peace, happiness - an overall sense of well-being. This happens all by itself. And yet, there's another option available that the awakened know: If we refrain from labeling our experience in terms of our biases, likes and dislikes… we meet the moment as it is.

It becomes simply energy moving through, and not something we need to run from or grasp. Instead of working against the law of our experience, the awakened know if what we pay attention to expands, we are wise to see the intelligence of paying attention to the "good half," while accepting the potential of sensing the "bad half" arising, for they can't be separated. The cool part is that once this is finally seen, without any doubt whatsoever, this too, happens by itself. In other words, choosing to pay attention to the more ideal half isn't needed; because you saw through illusion, flow happens - and you're in it. In truth, you *are* it.

Sensing the much greater wisdom in our hearts than our minds, we trust in our being and let it to guide the way; we allow it to dictate our next move. No longer coming from the dictates of our minds, we access a deeper wisdom that allows ourselves to be in harmony with life and its natural perfection, as it is. As a result, we're no longer concerned with what it looks like or how it will turn out; we're able to meet the next moment in an uncluttered and unfettered way. It's that simple.

Wisdom sees that if we just allow experience to be as it is, without labeling it, something else begins to happen. The wisdom of insecurity invites us *not* to cling to anything, not just because what we cling to we're bound by, but because absolutely nothing remains. Similarly, there's wisdom in no escape, too. When we understand that whatever is arising cannot arise and unfold in any other way than it actually does, wisdom blooms like the sun-drenched flower after a prolonged period of rain and clouds. *When we open our eyes and understand our situation, without any bias or agenda, wisdom moves within us – dancing with and to whatever's arising.* We find ourselves moving in rhythm to the circumstances and conditions of our lives, even if they appear asymmetrical and chaotic.

Inexplicably, we find ourselves responding to life in a way that we only imagined before. There's a flow present now, a flow that we always suspected was there, but didn't know how to align ourselves with. And with this flow comes greater ease, less stress and struggle. No longer opposing life, no longer seeing ourselves as "imperfect" and in need of fixing, we feel like a bird just let out of its cage. Our shackles are broken in two. Where we were once bound, now we're free. Like an orange must produce orange juice when it's squeezed, compassion oozes from us when we're squeezed, spilling onto those around us.

We discover that there's an ultimate reward for no longer engaging in self-deception; there's an ultimate reward for having absolute and full integrity. It's called freedom – freedom from the tyranny of the mind's ongoing insistence that it is the sole arbiter of reality, and that its unique view is the genuine article. No longer identified with the contents of the mind, we are freed from the negative emotions generated *by* that identification. And you laugh your head off. You laugh at how long you fooled yourself – and you revel in the feeling of a great burden that's been lifted. Suddenly you know why the Buddha was laughing so hard. You feel gratitude and relief. Once you really *see*, you never un-see.

Life then, is a celebration and a glorious opportunity to express our divinity, to choose whatever aspects of ourselves we wish to experience, while embracing those parts of ourselves that we'd prefer be hidden on the sidelines. In that embracing of both halves, the less desired half has a natural tendency to want to stay on the sidelines – and that's fine with us. If these aspects do end up presenting themselves from time to time, it's not a problem unless and until we make it a problem. Living in a world of opposites that arise together, we are grateful. We are fully aware that if misery wasn't a potential experience, we could never experience enjoyment. But first, we must look until we see.

Without pain and suffering, there is no joy and happiness. Without the willingness to feel insecure and vulnerable, there is no chance to experience the security and stability that comes from true understanding. Without hate, there's no love, and without sadness, there's simply no happiness. In other words, *we work with ourselves* because we know and accept the reality of our situation and how our experience unfolds. If we couldn't experience the so-called "lower" aspects of ourselves - those that we used to deem "imperfect" or "flawed," then in truth, we literally wouldn't have the ability to express and experience our natural strengths and gifts, either. I am here to express and enjoy. How about you?

The restoration of true perception lies in knowing that ultimate reality is a union of opposites. This knowing comes from seeing what's true in your direct experience - beyond belief - and beyond what others have told you. Therefore, the solution to the war of opposites demands the giving up of all boundaries - and not just the chaotic dance between the opposites against each other. Cutting out the root cause of our battle with the opposites is equal to seeing all boundaries as illusory. In Western terms, being "freed from the pairs of opposites," is the realization of the Kingdom of Heaven on Earth, despite the majority of the popular theologians and evangelists forgetting this.

Mainstream religion would have you believe that Heaven is a state of all positives, without any negatives, and not the true state that Heaven is the realization of "no-opposites" or "not-two-ness." In The Gospel of Thomas: We hear the words of Jesus when he said, *"When you make the two into one, and when you make the inner like the outer and the outer like the inner, and the upper like the lower, and when you make male and female into a single one, so that the male will not be male nor the female be female, then you enter the Kingdom."*

In my denial of the bad half, not only do I encourage it to stick around, I suppress the good half - what I prefer - from arising. When life knows we've seen it's a game of inclusion, the more our experience will accurately reflect that understanding. Seeing this, we welcome all aspects of ourselves, as they are. We watch the old existential discomfort that naturally arose from ignorance, dissolve from our experience. In its place, we can't help but notice the much greater sense of genuine gratitude arising for ALL of it, as it is - and not just the desired half.

The nature of reality and how it operates in us is simple - beyond all mental comprehension. If you don't yet see, do not be concerned. You will see when you see, as long as you continue to look to see what's actual. Always start where you are, not where you think you should be. There is no one keeping score; the more relaxed you are, the better off you are. There is no one workable approach for everyone here; there isn't a one-size fits all formula, either.

Nonetheless, this is an intimate and fruitful dance well worth dancing. Just put on your dancing shoes.

Chapter 6
Addiction & Grace

"O Lord, help me to be pure, but not yet."

~ **Saint Augustine**

When I was in the drafting stage of writing this book on imperfection, it occurred to me that it wouldn't be complete if I didn't discuss addiction. I mean, don't we see our addictions as imperfections? If you don't see the relationship between battling imperfections with addiction and grace, it is my hope that you soon will. Although I could very easily write a whole book on the subject, I felt for the purposes of this book, that dedicating an entire chapter on addiction would suffice. Since we know that every concept and experience has an opposing side, grace will be discussed as it relates to addiction, and how it arises in conjunction *with* addiction. Keep in mind that I don't have any degrees or letters behind my name in regards to addiction, but I do have a PHD in battling them!

The majority of them (especially the more harmful ones) are in my rear view mirror (knock on wood) but I still have a few I'm willing to share with you. I literally have no shame about any of them and some may have a problem with that. Oh, well. I am human and they come with the package. It is my sincere hope to shed some light on the nature of addiction - as I see it - and how grace, the most powerful force in the universe, fits in.

While the words here certainly don't classify as authoritative by any means, they accurately reflect my experience with both my struggles with addiction, and my acceptance of what arises with it, grace. Mere conceptual understanding won't ever deliver us from addiction, but it *can* help us to appreciate the transcending power of grace. And so, I ask you to read these words in a way that allows them to penetrate your heart and mind, resonating with you in the way it will, in your own experience.

What does it mean to be addicted, and when do we know we're addicted to something or someone, as opposed to when we're truly passionate and deeply interested in something or someone?

How do we distinguish love and need? Is there such a thing as a "healthy" addiction, or are we just fooling ourselves in an attempt to simply continue the behaviors we have a love/hate relationship with? When we think or hear of the word "addiction" we normally think of it in terms of being hooked on a chemical substance like heroin, cocaine, marijuana, prescription pills and perhaps the most damaging drug of all, alcohol.

It's interesting that the most "socially accepted" drug listed above, alcohol, is the one that does the most damage, ruining more individuals and families than all the others combined. Do you suppose there's a direct relationship here? I sure think so. As I mentioned in the introduction, I am a recovering alcoholic. I will never forget the morning of October 22, 1999. After a night of heavy drinking that started early, I awoke to not only a major headache, but to something within me that just knew it was over. As I stumbled into bed that night, I didn't intend on surrendering the next day, and yet it would be an understatement to say that I wasn't very open to surrendering.

I was totally unaware that the events of the next day would forever change me deeply.

Something ineffable (but very palpable) descended upon me, arming me with a deep realization that I had reached the end of the line - and that I was utterly and completely defeated. Somehow, I had finally reached my lowest emotional and spiritual bottom. To continue drinking was paramount to death, at least emotional and spiritually. At 35, I just wasn't ready to die.

I don't have the greatest memory, but I remember that morning as if it was yesterday. I always sensed that surrender had to be the way out, but until then, I wasn't ready to hand it over. That morning, in my absolute devastation and brokenness, the wholeness of reality washed over me in waves. I felt completely held in its infinite and unconditionally loving embrace - and I knew I'd never be the same again. There was a deep compassion that welled up within me. Indeed, grace happened and it clearly wasn't a result of any conscious decision or anything I earned. In every single fiber of my being, I knew my desire to drink was lifted. The desire to engage in the behavior that brought so much pain was removed - and it never came back.

Not everyone has their desire to drink lifted, so I have great compassion for those who can't shake the obsession to use. Grace made me humble. When you see the reality of the situation, humility is really only the appropriate response. Like any other alcoholic, I know I'm one drink away from inviting those destructive behaviors back. I can't take any credit for it, so I don't. In fact, I can't. I didn't do any of it.

The reality is addictions aren't just limited to substances, chemicals and foods. We're addicted to things like control, fear, projecting a certain image, staying at a certain weight, approval, work performance, success, love, infatuation, sex, and sex on drugs. Many are addicted to certain patterns and ways of thinking, including negativity and pessimism. If we look and see, we notice we get certain payoffs. In our insecurity and vulnerability, we're even addicted to perfection. Some of us are addicted to avoiding our perceived imperfections, running from them or compensating for them in a way others notice. We become obsessed with being preoccupied with aspects of ourselves we'd rather not face, and then wonder why we can't ever fulfill our deeper desires we sense will bring us the contentment we seek.

In this age of technology and instant information at our fingertips, many of us are addicted to Facebook, television, music, video games, mobile devices and porn. In the last decade, I have "picked up" a few addictions along the way. I'm addicted to checking my email, constantly surfing the net for the latest news (I look at basically the same 8 to 10 sites each day) and checking my cell phone throughout my day. For the record, if I text you, I want you to text me back within twenty minutes or so … or else I get impatient and even annoyed. You got that? LOL. One of Robocop's archenemies only gave his enemies "twenty seconds to comply." Heck, I'm being much more generous. I'm giving you twenty minutes to comply!

It's as if I latched onto the idea that texting is like the express checkout line at the supermarket. What's the point of having an "express line" if it isn't quick and convenient? Similarly, what's the point of texting if you're not going to get right back to me? Why can't you get right back to me when I text you? It's fast, easy and super-convenient, like the express checkout line, is it not? Granted, I know that I can never know if you got my text as soon as I sent it, and I can't know if your phone is even on your person or within earshot. I can't know if you're actually busy doing something more pressing, but even though I am aware of these things, it doesn't always seem to register. Come on, what's the delay? Are you avoiding me on purpose just to mess with me? Is my text unimportant to you? Do I humor you?

While I also realize it's my expectations and not the slow reply that causes my annoyance, it doesn't always help. At any rate, these pre-occupations don't really impact the quality of my life or my degree of happiness, so for the moment, I am okay with them. Who knows what tomorrow brings? Hold on for a second, I must go check my email - be right back. Just kidding.

To be human is to be addicted. Most humans are pretty intelligent with the ability to discern, evaluate, compare and distinguish. Unlike any other species we know of, humans have the capacity to not only be self-aware, but to reflect on their present experience - and alter their future course if they so choose. Despite the ability to discern, evaluate and judge, humanity is challenged when it comes to fully recognizing the difference between truth and illusion. We can say all along it's been our Achilles heel, coded in our DNA. In our wholehearted willingness to admit this, we surrender to our situation and become more aware of the many instances where we're addicted.

Readily admitting that we have a tendency to be easily seduced by the senses, we give ourselves a greater degree of vigilance and discernment. Like Jesus, Socrates was put to death for attempting to teach the importance and value of discernment saying things like, *"Obscurity is dispelled by augmenting the light of discernment, not by attacking the darkness."* In this world of duality, we are fortunate to possess the awareness to immediately detect what doesn't serve us by noticing how our bodies react to the presence of certain sensation and stimuli. Truth is simple and our bodies are not to be ignored if we want harmony. Being aware of and avoiding these types of sensation and stimuli is all that's really required for us to ultimately transcend these destructive forces.

Addiction attaches desire and imprisons the energy of desire to certain behaviors, things or people. Consequently, these objects of attachment become obsessions and preoccupations, stealing our capacity to be present in our own lives and in the lives of those we most love and care about. This attachment nails our desires (in a laser-like fashion) to people, specific behaviors or ways of thinking - and creates addiction. The very same forces responsible for addiction to substances like alcohol and drugs are also responsible for our addiction to ideas, beliefs, moods and patterns of thinking. We find ourselves in bondage, in a hypnotic entrancement of our own making, and yet, paradoxically, our addictions are virtually beyond our control. Many people still think it's a matter of choice whether we drink too much, smoke too much or beat ourselves up too much.

But upon closer examination, it's not too difficult to see that we aren't pulling our own strings. Yes, it appears that way, but if we dig deeper, we see that we're not the Master puppeteer after all. It's as if our will has been hijacked, conditioned to engage in ways of thinking or behaving that isn't for our highest good. As I stated in my book, *"Born To Be Happy – How to Uncover Your Natural State of Happiness,"* "If happiness is really a choice, why would we ever choose to be unhappy?" Why would we intentionally engage in thoughts and behaviors that bring pain and suffering?

Like the man behind the curtain in The Wizard of Oz, there's more than meets the eye when we delve deeper. When we pull back the curtains, we see we aren't pulling the control levers. We notice forces and energies that are happening spontaneously and without our conscious intention. Addiction isn't something we can easily rid ourselves of with our intellectual capacity, or by applying some simple remedy or strategy, for it is in the very nature of addiction to prey on our attempts to control or master it! There isn't any cookie-cutter solution that will cure what ails us. There is a cunningly deceptive intelligence to addiction - and it has no boundaries or lengths it won't go to. Integrity and dignity are the last things it cares about. It will take over the person with the lowest IQ just as easily as the person with the highest IQ.

It's sitting on our shoulder, and its voice can be heard mostly in times when we seek to soothe ourselves, or run from something we'd rather not face. Our object of desire (whether a substance, a behavior or way of thinking or perceiving) whispers in our ear, convincing us to call upon it in our time of need. In our more conscious moments, we may think it all the way through, perhaps refraining from engagement *this* time, but as long as we think we're ultimately in control, it's only a matter of time before we heed its call and empty promises. In a zombie-like state, we find ourselves hopping on the familiar wheel of suffering, spinning around, experiencing the inevitable highs and lows that ensue. Until we really *see* this, we forever remain in its grips, allowing the addiction to remain in control.

Self-deception and denial, two of the most influential factors/symptoms of addiction, brings more darkness and ignorance. Surrendering and admitting defeat dispels darkness, and enlightens us. It's the difference between the attitudes of "I can do this all by myself" to "I cannot do this alone." It's the difference between will and pride to willingness and humility. Our orientation makes all the difference. Allowing our intellect to entertain its delusions of grandeur - along with its ability to "know" what's best, we forever remain in the dark to the causes of our afflictions. Our intellect dreams up, and then comfortably bathes in a wide variety of plausible excuses, justifications and minimizations. Simultaneously, it remains *uncomfortably* hypnotized by these very forces, leading us to further engage in these habitual behaviors.

When willpower is all that is present, desire ultimately wins. When willpower is busy at the wheel, we're in the backseat thinking we're driving. What's remarkable is that even if we intellectually recognize that our behavior is self-destructive and possessing a downward spiral effect, this recognition often has *no deterring impact whatsoever* - even though we often think it does. It is only when we humbly recognize that our way doesn't work that we begin to figure out that a kinder, gentler approach (based in reality) is needed. This approach includes faith in a brighter future, deep humility, and an unreserved acceptance of our present lot. Intellectual knowledge and honest admittance of our addiction(s) has never given us the power to control them or make them go away. It's only a good first step - and a critical one at that.

Wisdom clearly shows us that serving two masters never works, at least not in the long run. We can hear the words of Jesus when he said, *"A slave cannot serve two masters, otherwise that slave will honor the one and offend the other."* We hang on as long as we can, trading short-term pleasure for long-term pain. And we tell ourselves (and those concerned for us) we're choosing the behavior!

Since absolutely everything is energy, inherent in any thought, intention, belief, or behavior is a vibration - and that distinct vibration has a distinct and corollary vibration that determines our experience.

In other words, if I choose a behavior, I also choose the consequence. It's that duality working again. Wisdom clearly shows us that we can only serve one master, heaven or hell, but not both. We *can* serve both, but the wisdom of no escape demands we must suffer the consequences. Hell is the inevitable byproduct of choosing the behaviors that divide and fracture - and not something imposed on us by a punitive and judgmental God. Heaven is the inevitable consequence of the decisions and behaviors already in harmony with nature and the law of our experience - and dare I say, a life living in "perfect contentment" ... where nothing needs to be added or subtracted.

It's no secret that groups like AA, NA and OA (Overeaters Anonymous) all maintain that if there's any hope for the addict, one must hoist up the white flag and admit complete and absolute defeat. Step one of the 12-Step program, says, *"We admitted we are powerless over alcohol (or drugs, food or whatever) and that our lives had become unmanageable."* Unless we voluntarily take this crucial first step, nothing changes. Excuse the crass metaphor, but I really like the visual: until we take this step, and *mean* it, we're just pissing in the wind - often a gale force wind! Wisdom sees that the person who seeks support is acting from strength, not weakness. Ego sees the opposite - and yet we believe ego is on our side.

Wisdom blooms when that person thanks its ego for sharing, and then in humility, gets that support for as long as it takes. That's integrity, knowing what you need in the moment. No man is an island. There's something very attractive about real humility. Prideful people certainly don't understand the transcending power of paradox; they are too identified with thinking they know what's best, fearing what they imagine might happen if they don't know. Simply put, they're looking in the wrong direction. They unwittingly attempt to hide the ego's fragility, not only to themselves, but to others as well. Until they get honest, they won't ever stop running. They will continue to be chased by the very thing they want to be delivered from.

Allow me to interject something very important here: If there's only one thing that you take away from this book, I would wish for you to see how critical it is to understand the true nature of paradoxes – and how they operate in your life. Granted, this was the topic of chapter four, but the paradoxes in addiction are essential to understand. I would wish for you to see how your mind naturally resists paradoxes, and how to best orient yourself in such a way that you live in harmony with your own experience … all with the mind's assistance. Your mind can be a wonderful servant, but only if you use it correctly. If you don't, you are its slave.

Once you truly understand paradoxes, and once you see how they operate in and through almost every aspect of your life, then you'll notice you're also in perfect harmony with Life, for they are one and the same. I can't possibly overstate the significance of this understanding. It can only be seen and realized when you examine for yourself. Look until you see. Don't just "get this" conceptually. Keep going.

Conceptual understanding is limited, and therefore, doesn't constitute real knowing. You "get this" when you experience the transformational power of understanding (and living from) the paradoxes, experientially. This is when you know. This is the knowing that transforms.

Enlightened beings have all conveyed the same thing: the vast majority of the human population is "trapped within a dream," driven by unseen forces and tendencies that creates division that must alienate and fracture. Being unaware of this phenomenon, humans typically continue to suffer for the greater portion of their lives. Like a sentimental handmade quilt or scarf we inherited from Grandma, we don't want to give up our ways, even though they hurt. We are creatures of habit; we like what's comfortable, even it it's not working. We pray to God to help us experience relief from the burden of our sins. We go to confession in the hopes of alleviating the guilt, shame and remorse we can't seem to shake.

We conclude that salvation seems to be for the lucky few, but not for us. What often takes a backseat is remembrance of the transformative power of positive thinking and detachment from negative thinking *as* a doorway to transcendence. We lose sight of the knowing sense that compassion, too, is the doorway to grace. We walk around in a trance-like state, mostly repeating the same thoughts, beliefs and behaviors. Somehow we find ourselves in a very tenuous situation, strapped with this limited and dissatisfied mind that continues to torture us - yet on some level, we seem to enjoy creating all the drama it provides.

We don't recall ever asking to come into this human form with all its challenges, sorrows and eventual demise; we don't recall asking for our particular set of parents, especially through the "my parents really annoy me stage." And we definitely don't remember the meaning of it all! Our main struggle in life then, appears to be a vain attempt to rise above this confounded and painful mystery we're seemingly enveloped in. Yet inwardly, we sense that mysteries aren't to be solved, but lived and surrendered to. In truth, the traditional resolutions of love and prayer are still validated scientifically in our experience. What we entertain and engage in, we must experience.

Until we see that we already possess within ourselves the power of our own salvation (through grace and our willingness to surrender) we remain stuck, just like Winnie the Pooh in the rabbit hole, without any honey in sight. Not only are we unable to fulfill our desires that we sense will bring us contentment, we often ignore those desires to do so. Like the unpopular schoolboy forced to the back of the bus, our truer desires are pushed back for "some time in the future" when we have our act together.

We live life on the layaway plan, acting as if it's a dress rehearsal. The longings in our hearts disappear from our conscious awareness and its energy usurped by forces that are not at all compassionate and loving. In fact, our desires are shackled and we give ourselves over to things, that in our moments of real honesty, we don't want. In our unconsciousness entrancement, we somehow become willing partners with our addiction - and *literally trade* the peace and happiness we really want for continued engagement in the very activities and consequences we *don't* want.

The adage, "we can never get enough of what we don't really want" rings true and becomes our living reality. We become numb to the fact that we can't ever separate the behaviors from the repercussions - and despite what Pink Floyd might claim, it isn't always comfortable. As the Apostle Paul said so succinctly, *"I do not understand my own behavior; I do not act as I mean to, but I do the things I hate. Though the will to do what is good is in me, the power to do is not; the good thing I want to do, I never do; the evil thing which I do not want – that is what I do."*

Even before the time of Jesus, we've intimately known of our limited human nature, and yet somehow, we haven't been able to connect the dots staring right at us. In its infinite "wisdom", the mind still thinks it knows best. It is this mistaken conclusion that overshadows the seeing that our *weaknesses,* as they are, are meant to be with us, and can lead us to a deeper appreciation of grace and surrender. In fact, they can render us powerless, bringing us to our knees. It is this letting go that renders us powerful. It is *this* very condition of being on our knees when grace reveals itself, and either eases our burden, or permanently removes our obsession to that which enslaved us.

This once-seen enemy to our human freedom (that breeds willfulness and attempts to control) is the very doorway to our salvation. Because it forces us to worship objects of attachment, addiction forces us to isolate and alienate ourselves from each other. This prevents us from freely loving others and ourselves. It eats away at our integrity and dignity. Personally, I know very good-hearted and intelligent people "in the know," possessing a lot of common sense, but don't yet see the essential paradoxes that would free them.

What often goes unnoticed is the glue that holds it together. Addictive negative patterns of thinking, lack of humility and self-deception is that glue. They don't yet see that the way to win is to give in, to hoist up the white flag once and for all. Willful pride is in the driver's seat and grace is in the backseat, patiently waiting to be called on. I suspect that shame and guilt play a large role, too. Fear of facing who they think they'd be if they surrendered can be a real barrier. It's not real, but it feels real.

Taking responsibility for other's challenges, even if it's your own grown children you love and adore, is a symptom of misunderstanding how it all really works. Most of all, identification with the contents of the mind plays the most significant role.

Since illusion is the second most powerful force (behind grace) in the world, this can be difficult to see. Being enmeshed with the contents of the mind is easy; noticing you aren't the mind and its contents is not so easy. Nonetheless, it's the difference that determines the quality of one's life. Even though we're conditioned biologically to seek pleasure and avoid pain (as a function of survival) ...having complex human brains, we get carried away into the psychological realm. Imaginary forces, mostly driven by irrational fears and misdirected desires take hold. Fortunately, it all crumbles when we clearly see through illusion.

The more we seek pleasure and avoid pain, the more painful it gets. It's like having poison sumac and thinking that scratching will make it better. The more we itch, the more it spreads. The temporary highs are followed by excruciating lows - and the compulsive cycle strengthens. Faced with painful stories about our so-called imperfections or real disabilities, our upbringing, uncomfortable feelings like pain, hurt, anxiety, numbness, apathy and withdrawal, the tendency to want to alleviate these feelings arises … and we're back engaging in the very behaviors that keep us down.

So how do we invite grace into our lives in such a way as to actually feel it moving through us? How do we invite grace into our experience and let it know it's a welcome guest, free to stay as long as it wants? Grace comes in a variety of forms. It comes in the form of an insight, an understanding, an opening of our hearts and minds … or the experience of being totally broken. We've all had very difficult times in our lives and when we look back, even though we remember feeling hopeless and confused, we see we somehow made it through. We also recognize that it was in those times where we transformed the most. We can say anything that helps us cope better is grace.

Any time we experience compassion and embracing something or someone, grace is operating in us - especially if we found it extremely difficult to open to that something or someone previously. Where we once had real difficulty trusting, now we can trust. That's grace. But first, we must be willing *to* trust. Sometimes grace is very subtle and difficult to sense. Sometimes it's fierce and comes in the form of a sledgehammer, and sometimes it is soft and tender. Grace blossoms when we see that we really aren't ultimately in control our lives, and that something far greater than our limited and finite minds can perceive or understand is essentially in control. Anyone who ever drove home during a blackout knows this.

Most people who suffer from drug and/or alcohol addiction will tell you that fighting addiction is like fighting a grisly bear. What sane person would fight a grisly bear? What are the odds of survival? What are the odds of winning a battle with a grisly bear? I don't know about you, but if I suddenly encountered a grisly bear, I'd immediately get into a subservient position and play dead. I'd offer no resistance whatsoever. When the bear noticed there wouldn't be any opposition, or threat, there's a very good chance I'd be left alone. Addiction is like this. Anytime we go to battle with addiction, we lose. When we fight addiction, it sees your resistance as opposition, and therefore, a threat to its survival.

Like the bear, it won't back down. In fact, in order to continue to survive, it'll fight back even harder. But if we get down on our knees and give in to it, we take the fight right out of it. Don't be insane; don't ever fight a grisly bear - or your addiction. Never is it a fair fight. It's a losing battle, every time. Sane people know the reality of their situation. Sane people don't fight what ails them.

Thinking and believing that we are in control of our lives is perhaps the greatest obstacle to accepting the grace that's ever-present, all the time. When we turn our lives over to that which is greater than us, that which is cradling us all the time, only then can we feel its power and presence in our lives. Even though we can't fool grace, real prayer from the heart can be an effective way to invite grace into our life. Grace knows when we're being phony, and it knows when we're being self-serving. When we say to whoever we understand to be our higher power, "Your will, not mine," or "Give me whatever I need to get through this," we're inviting grace into our lives.

When we sincerely say something similar to what Francis of Assisi said, "Give me what I need to see, Lord, so that I may be an instrument for your peace and love on this earth; whatever it takes, Lord, I am willing to do" - and mean it, we're inviting grace to move within us. Is there any way out of being so attached to the way we view things, including ourselves? Is there a way to finally and fully embrace both our strengths *and* weaknesses? Can we just "opt out" like we can when we click the link at the bottom of an email, notifying the sender to unsubscribe us? Can we remove ourselves from the situation and unsubscribe from that thing, behavior, thought or belief that causes us stress?

In a very certain sense, yes, we most definitely can - but we must go about it in the way that works, using our good sense. "Removing ourselves" is just what we do - but perhaps not in the way you might think, and certainly not in the sense of running away or disassociating. As I like to remind, in order to understand something, we must first be aware. So, we must first see the particular thing, pattern of thinking or behavior that causes our struggle. Can I ask you to think of something right now that causes you ongoing stress and strain? Do you have this specific thing in your mind? Okay, now that you do, doesn't it make sense that in order to transcend it, you must learn how to be with it in a very different way than before - and perhaps learn how to dance in sync with it so as not to step on its toes?

In other words, can you learn how to *be* or *dance with* this itch in your mind, without scratching it? In order to do this, you'd have to be more conscious, present and awake to its movements and tendencies within you, agreed? If so, that means you must toss out running, justifying, minimizing, judging, comparing, beating yourself up and resisting *as* a strategy to transcend, right? *Expecting* perfection goes right out the window, too, doesn't it?

Naturally, if we want to recover from a certain addiction, or as Whitman says, "dismiss what insults our soul" - then it stands to reason that coming out of our hypnotic, trance-like state (that invited our affliction) involves us being more aware than before. We must learn how to be with these uncomfortable, yet familiar sensations in a way where we don't run and hide, space out or numb out. As Jesus said in the Gospel of Thomas, *"Know what is in front of your face, and what is hidden from you will be disclosed to you."*

This dance involves us shifting our attention from control to surrender, from dis-ease to ease.

Without focusing on a particular result, we remove from the dance, all our conclusions and expectations, all our attachment to our painful stories - and we dance with what is. Putting on our new dancing shoes, we trust in being, knowing that our mind doesn't have the ultimate solution. If the mind steps in and asks how, we respond, "Simply by letting go of the struggle, right now, that's how." We notice that what we pay attention to expands. Therefore, if we pay attention to and resist only the "bad" side of our affliction (even though both sides arise together) we won't get to experience the "good" side that ultimately frees us from enslavement.

If addiction and grace do indeed arise together, you give up everything you *think* you know about how to go about it. You let go, right now, any and all effort to try to escape the condition you find yourself in. It is only when we allow ourselves NOT to know that a new potential can arise. But hey, don't believe me. The opposite of willfulness and pride is surrender and humility. The opposite of control is letting go. Without any intent to fix our selves, you openly and innocently meet your situation as it is, without wishing it would go away or be any different than it is. You simply notice how the mind still seeks to control the situation and tell you what's best. You can just acknowledge the mind for its input, without identifying with it.

Silently you say, "Thanks for sharing, but let me try looking this way." Without any intent to "do" anything at all, you're just present and aware, making no conclusions at all. You may experience some confusion initially, but you aren't concerned with understanding what's happening or how it will happen; that's just more mind seeking control. Understanding will come in time, and it will be the kind from below the neck, where wisdom resides. What you *are* concerned with is dancing face-to-face, and eye-to-eye - an intimate look. If you're confused or trying to understand, you relax and see that the awareness *of* confusion isn't confused - and that the awareness *of* trying to understand isn't trying to understand.

We think our lives are so important, and everything comes to mean so much. In one sense they are, and in another they aren't at all. As a result, we tighten up. In doing so, we remove ourselves from the flow and simplicity of life. However, we can just rest - and trust that when life moves us to move in a certain way, we'll move. We rest in the knowing sense that absolutely everything is perfectly okay as it is; we know and trust that what's *presently arising* in our experience cannot be any other way. What already arose couldn't have been any different, either. We laugh at our mind when it tries to convince us otherwise - that we *could have* or *should have known better,* and therefore, *could have* or *should have done better.*

It's all fit and fury, leading to nothing but unnecessary pain and suffering. In another sense, the desire to recover is also perfect - and falling or relapsing *during* that recovery is also perfect - all to the point where nothing needs to be added to or subtracted from. We're moving in perfect harmony, because in both senses, we're in sync. It's only our mind that tells us different - and we believed it. It's easy to forget that we're essentially all the same, just disguised differently, animated by the same source.

It's easy to forget that, in reality, we're merely small specks in the grand scheme of things, just passing through. If you don't yet see it's happening quickly, look again. We are a parenthesis in Eternity, here today, gone tomorrow. Although we can never know exactly what another is going through, we can be assured one thing for sure - and that is this: though another's particulars struggle appears different than ours, they arise from the same source. That source doesn't believe in the labels and descriptions *we* place on people, places and things - but it allows it. And what one man sees as imperfection, another sees as perfection. In closing, enjoy this poignant story from the Jewish tradition:

For a whole year I felt the longing to go to my Rabbi Bunan and talk to him. But every time I entered the house

I felt I wasn't man enough. Once though, as I was walking across a field and weeping, I knew that I must run to the Rabbi without delay. He asked, "Why are you weeping?" I answered, "I am after all alive in this world, a being created with all its senses and limbs, but I do not know what it is that I was created for and what I am good for in this world." "Little fool," he replied, "that's the same question that I have carried around with me all my life. You will come and eat the evening meal with me today."

Chapter 7
Hey, It's Just a Ride

"The world is like a ride at an amusement park, and when you choose to go on it, you think it's real, because that's how powerful our minds are. And it's fun, for a while. Some people have been on the ride for a long time, and they begin to question: 'Is this real or is this just a ride?' And other people have remembered, and they come back to us and they say, 'Hey, don't worry, don't be afraid – ever – because this is just a ride!' AND WE KILL THOSE PEOPLE."

~ Bill Hicks (1961-1994)

I really get a kick out of the chapter illustration because it perfectly expresses a favorite metaphor of mine. Imagine that you've been tossed from an airplane flying at 38,000 feet - and you have no parachute. You didn't ask to be tossed; you were just tossed. There's nothing at all you can do about that. As you're falling towards the earth, you consider your options. Seeing that you *will* impact the ground - and most likely splat - you see that you really only have two options. What are those options?

They're essentially depicted by the two characters riding together on the roller coaster ride: You can either be absolutely frightened, worried, try to fix it, alter it to your liking, control it, improve upon it or try to make it end, OR ... seeing that it's just a ride, you can simply enjoy it! After all, you have 38,000 feet to let go and rest in the most amazing experience you've ever had. This basically sums up life. You're already here, right? Even though you didn't ask to be here, you're already here. Indeed, you were born, and for certain, you're going to die. With birth comes death. It's that duality thing again.

While we're constantly reminded of the fact of our own mortality, we somehow push this fact as far away on the periphery as we can, thinking since it's not a good thing, the further the better. The truth is, it's neither a good or bad thing; it just is. At some particular point in time, whether it's a few moments from now or years from now, we won't be here anymore. One day we'll be six feet under, dead as a doornail, deep fried, taking a dirt nap, or in this metaphor, a big splatter on the ground.

Keeping this in mind, wouldn't we have a better appreciation for each day we wake up? I get a friendly reminder each day I drive up my driveway. To the left is a very old cemetery. It's that close, and I love it. (My dog Molly loves it, too.) Go look at the picture again. Which rider are you? Are you the relaxed rider who realizes the inevitable moment can't be any different - and thus enjoys the ride, or are you the uptight, fearful rider who clings to the notion that something other should or could be happening - and thus resists - and doesn't really enjoy the ride?

Let's examine this from a different perspective. When it comes to how you live your life, can you say *how* you go about it and why? Where do your intentions come from and what are they based in? How seriously do you take your life? Are you being driven by some compelling need or desire? Are you perhaps spending your attention and energy towards living the most perfect life that you can imagine - one that *others* would surely respect and admire? Is your life a direct manifestation of trying to live in such a way that it conforms to some ideal of what you "think" it should be?

What might be different if you had the "mind over matter" attitude - that if you don't mind, it doesn't matter? What might be different if you had the attitude that "what you think of me is none of my business?" What's fortunate is that most of us have the ability to live our lives as we desire. If we want enlightenment, great wealth, notoriety, recognition or fame, we can have that. No one is stopping us from achieving all that - and those things are all fine. But in going after those things, we do well to remember that it's just a ride! It may or may not happen according to plan, but when we know it's just a ride, we can enjoy it, wherever it ends up!

Although it certainly *appears* as if we do, we really don't have control over most of it anyway. In the end, what will it all ultimately mean? In the end, we already know the eventual outcome, don't we? What will we really "have" as a result? Won't we be one big splatter on the ground as soon as the ride is over? Ashes to ashes and dust to dust, right? Can we do anything about what's naturally going to occur? Won't we join the billions that have passed on before us? And so, if there is anything really worth "accomplishing" in life, don't you think the most worthy endeavor would be to just enjoy the ride - whatever YOUR ride looks like?

What is the purpose of *your* life? Have you really broken it down to the bare essentials, according to what you most value? Do your actions actually reflect your values? Have you distilled it down and crystallized your purpose? Without a clear target, we have nothing to aim for, right? We'd be like archers, bow and arrow in hand, with no bulls-eye in sight, basically suffering the slings and arrows of outrageous misfortune, wouldn't we? We'd basically be a rudderless ship, without any ability to successfully navigate to our intended destination.

There are many ways to enjoy our lives; one person's idea of enjoyment may be another's idea of misery. However, there are certain facts in life that we'd ALL do well to acknowledge and enjoy - because there's absolutely nothing we can do about them. For example, basically each person lives according to their own desires and interpretations of how things are - and how they'd like things to be. Based on self-interest, most people are essentially dialed into the WIFM channel - the "what's in it for me" channel. Having close to 7 billion channels being simultaneously tuned into one big network, there's bound to be lots of static created from all the opposing frequencies working against each other.

Your channel may be tuned into being in service to others and my channel might be tuned into taking from others. Your channel may be tuned into helping organize the chaos in other people's lives and mine might be tuned into making sure your agenda gets messed up. Most channels are tuned into controlling other people's channels with the hope they'll adhere more to their channel! As a result of so many agendas of self-interest, it's no wonder why competing frequencies don't match up.

If we can realize the intelligence and good sense of tuning our channels to the clearest and best signal called, "enjoy the ride no matter what" channel - and not take life so seriously, we won't experience all the static and confusion that most continue to experience. If we insist on taking our lives so seriously, we can still opt to enjoy taking our lives seriously! If we want to remain concerned about our lives and concerned about the lives of those we most love and care for, we can also enjoy being concerned about those we love and care for.

Whatever it is we decide to make our lives about - and whatever channel we tune into, whether it's considered "worthy" or "unworthy" by those around us, we enjoy it because we're doing what *we* want. Being given the freedom to live as we choose, we enjoy that freedom. In the end, if for whatever reason we can't seem to work out that simple formula for happiness, we can at least remember that hey, it's just a ride! You must watch this three-minute video clip of this very funny and irreverent late comic, Bill Hicks. You'll be glad you did. Simply google, "Bill Hicks It's Just a Ride."

Have you noticed that so many people find it very difficult to laugh at themselves? I mean, really laugh at themselves, the kind of hearty laugh that comes from the belly and not just the throat? And have you noticed the awkward moment when you're laughing at another's expense and you see that *they* aren't laughing? Why do we take ourselves so seriously? Why is it that we are quick to laugh at another's foibles but not our own? From my perspective, I'd have to say attachment to our ego prevents us really being comfortable and secure in our own skin. And since egos are generally fragile and need constant reinforcement, we don't like it when we're laughed at or have become the butt of a joke.

What's most unfortunate is our identification with ego as who we are. We have no problem expressing or playing to our strengths, but when it comes to our weaknesses, we'd rather not have them out on full display for all to see. If we liken ourselves to an art gallery having an exhibit, we're much more likely to pull out all our great works and leave all of our "embarrassing" or "messed up" works in the back room. It is in denial and ignorance of our dual nature (as finite human beings) that we get caught between the infinite and the limited, the light and the dark, the good and the bad, the grandeur and the misery.

In our ignorance and tendency to engage in self-deception, we deny our *both and* nature, and place ourselves in a disordered state of being. In order to be a Saint, one must first be a sinner. In order to be happy, one must first be sad. In order to be awake, one must first be asleep. In order to transcend the limits of our interpretations, one must first be mired *in* those limits. Those struggling with feeling good about who they are - warts and all - are operating under the illusion that they *should* be different than they are.

Granted, *you can* be different than you are, but not in this moment. You can only be as you already are in this moment. In another moment, you can be different, but not now. Wisdom sees the good sense of accepting who you are, right now - because if you don't, you only further entrench what you don't want. A preacher put this question to a class of children: *"If all the good people in the world were red and all the bad people were green, what color would you be?"* Little Jessica thought intensely for a moment and then her face lit up and she replied: *"Reverend, I'd be streaky!"* That's real wisdom from a child.

To think in terms of either or, teetering on the extremes of self-love and self-hate, aiming for perfection (because we have difficulty accepting our weaknesses) is paramount to keeping any real kind of contentment at bay. Splitting our selves in two, we find ourselves in a constant daily battle. In an ongoing struggle to be something we're not, and to achieve something we think will make us "happy", we face the opposite direction of where peace and fulfillment is found. Attempting to arrive at some place other than where we are guarantees discontent. Spending our attention and energy on trying to be the person others expect of us guarantees discontent.

It seldom occurs to us to just stop and rest, and look at where we are, and consider that just maybe everything is okay as it is. Maybe it's perfectly fine as it is, and that balance is found by relaxing into our dual nature - tuning into the channel that brings contentment. Seeing the reality of our situation - that we can only live from our dual nature, and that we already are living *from* our dual nature, we can relax in that knowing and notice what arises.

Only when we voluntarily recognize the nature of our situation are we able to respond in an intelligent and responsible way. Believing we are a victim of external forces and circumstances, carrying around a "woe is me" attitude will never induce the life we truly want. It's not rocket science. I don't want to speak for you, but I'd guess you're not different than most. All we really want is to be happy and enjoy life, right? By accepting and embracing BOTH halves of all of our characteristics - and knowing they arise together, we empower ourselves to allow happiness and enjoyment to arise in our experience.

If we chase after or strive for happiness, while suppressing our unhappiness, happiness will elude us. The paradox of happiness dictates that when we align ourselves with truth and not falsehood - and stop arguing with reality - our natural state of happiness can't help *but* arise. It's a deconstruction project, where we look and see what covers over our natural state of happiness. After all, we were born to be happy!

To be wholly unconcerned, yet intimately engaged, it is requisite that we live our lives engaged in whatever life is moving us to do, without concern whether we're doing it right or performing to our best ability. Since there are no mistakes, our peace and security lies in knowing we can't do it "wrong". In fact, there's no such thing as "doing it wrong." To be wholly unconcerned and intimately engaged means that we aren't preoccupied with how we're being perceived, what it looks like, and how it will turn out.

Being detached from our interpretations and meanings of things, we transfer all that energy towards just showing up fully, without insisting our agenda be met. Where we once erected all kinds of walls and barriers between our selves and the moment, we meet what's happening innocently and fresh, knowing any other way is pure insanity. Wisdom sees that unhappiness arises when we don't want what we have, and happiness arises when we want what we have.

Wholly unconcerned and intimately engaged, no longer do we lie to ourselves about our finitude and mortality. With life comes death and nothing will ever change this fact; we enjoy the relatively short time we have in this human form. In our moments of clarity, we see that the only appropriate response to life is gratitude, giving thanks for the act of seeing, hearing, tasting, feeling and breathing - and the experiences of pain and joy, sadness and happiness. As no two snowflakes are the same, we express and enjoy our dual nature that only we uniquely possess. When we were made, the mold was destroyed!

No longer do we misplace our responsibility for our own experience; we know we're responsible for all of it. No longer do we lie to ourselves about the richness and beauty of life. No longer do we project ourselves backward in guilt and forward in anxiety - and we let our fictions end. In place of our stories and fictions *about* existence, we live authentically in a state of open discovery, noticing when we attempt to delude ourselves. We face our fundamental obligation to find out what's true and real, without relying on any outside source to tell us what's true.

When we look at the beauty of say, a waterfall cascading down a lush gorge, or a majestic mountain peak covered in snow with the setting sun just beyond it, our breath is taken away. At first sight of this scenery, we have a tendency to gasp in awe. All other activity is suspended and we're simply aware, noticing our desire to simply take in what we see. In this seeing, we find ourselves resting in the beauty of the scene. We don't want anything *from* our object of affection; we find ourselves in deep gratitude just for the ability to see it. In this seeing, all grasping and egoic tendencies spontaneously dissolve and we are left relaxing into our basic and fundamental awareness.

Resting with the world, without any desire to change or fix it, all is perfect as it is. Much like grace, nature has a way of grabbing us against our will, thus suspending our will. We are ushered into a quiet clear space, free of desire, agitation and self-contraction. And in this space, where time is no longer sensed, we sense oneness with everything, without any boundary between our selves and what we see. The two are one - and there's not a snowballs chance in hell anyone could convince us otherwise.

In this quiet, open space where time is suspended, we find ourselves aware and totally present. In that moment, subtle revelations, deeper insights and flashes of higher truths may be revealed to us, stoking a fire inside that burns away anything unlike it. Temporarily transported from our daily lives, we revel in the magnificence of the scenery that removes any desire or need to have it any other way than it is. In fact, we are given a glimpse into what it's like to live in the timeless now, where no problems exist - where everything simply arises perfectly and completely.

It is in this calm moment of being in the eye of the storm where we realize that it is our mind that erects barriers, and judges what arises as good or bad, right or wrong. Without referring to thought to tell us about a thing, we see absolutely everything as already perfect the way it is. Nature reminds us, not so much by its scenery, but what it does *to* us and what it does *in* us: it steals our desire to be elsewhere.

This isn't merely an exercise in imagination. This is the real thing – the actual structure of the cosmos. This beauty pervades everything in the cosmos and it is only the mind that tells us a different story, a story based on what the five, limited sensory tools perceive. And then we believe perception is reality. It's like expecting an unawake man to explain the awakened perspective, or expecting a severely drunken man not to slur. No matter what explanation is given, it will never match reality. But what might happen if we could see the entire universe (and everything in it) as being immensely beautiful, like the exquisite scene in nature that suspends our will? What if we saw that every single arising, as it is, without exception, *as* an object of absolute beauty?

Just as the extraordinarily beautiful object in nature suspends our will, so too, would the contemplation of everything ordinary in the universe *as* an object of beauty, would open our awareness to the truth that whatever arises *is* as it should be. All of our running towards pleasure and away from pain would immediately come to rest - and through grace, our self-contraction lifted. When this happens, we discover that we naturally embrace *all* that we are.

Nature is the best teacher. Henry David Thoreau said nature never apologizes, and apparently it's because nature doesn't have any concept of right and wrong, ugly and beautiful and this and that. It's evident that some of the things we call "opposites" do appear to exist in nature. For example, there are big fish and small fish, large rocks and small rocks, mature trees and immature trees - with sickly leaves and healthy leaves. But it isn't problematic for them. It doesn't toss them into fits of rage or attacks of panic. Perhaps there are dumb hippos and smart hippos, but it doesn't seem to bother them much. You just don't find inferiority complexes in hippos.

Similarly, there is both life and death in nature, but it doesn't seem to terrify nature like it does humans. An old cat isn't caught up in fear and anxiety over its impending death. When its time has come, it gracefully moves to a secluded corner, curls up and goes to sleep one last time. An ill sparrow that knows its time is near, perches quietly on a branch and stares off into the distance at its last sunset. When it sees the light no more, it closes its eyes one final time, and without any drama or fanfare, falls gently to the ground below. It's all so natural.

What a stark contrast from the way most humans resist going into that good night, raging against the dying of the light! While pain and pleasure most certainly appear in nature, they never become problems to be concerned with. Dogs wag their tails in excitement when asked to go for a ride or a walk. When it experiences pain, it yelps. When not in any pain, it doesn't fret about it, nor is it concerned that it may come back later. It doesn't dread future pain and doesn't lament past pain. It's all a very natural and simple affair. We may say nature is just ignorant and doesn't know any better, but nature is far more intelligent than we'll ever be. Nature is not only smarter than we think - nature is smarter than we *can* think.

While many humans puff out their chests proclaiming to be the most intelligent species in the entire universe, nature humbly sits back and laughs knowing it produced the mind that claims that. Nature is label-free, forever lacking any desire to classify and discern all the numerous forms it displays. It doesn't need to say, "These animals look different from those animals, so let's call these animals *tigers* and these animals *giraffes*." Or, "Hurricanes are bad and do so much damage, but light rain showers are good for the growth of vegetables and flowers, so embracing light showers while resisting hurricanes is wise." No labels, no problems. No boundaries, no problems. No story, no suffering. Absolutely everything arises from the same source and is independent of any story or feeling about it.

Like nature, wanting absolutely nothing other than what actually arises, and wanting nothing other than what you are - as you are - you are timelessly frozen in paralysis by the sheer beauty and perfection that shows up all around you. Being released from past clinging to misguided notions that you couldn't seem to shake, you are freshly undone as one who made distinctions, however small. As Eckhart said, *"To have that consciousness where distinction never gazed"* is what you're operating from. Being in the world, but not of it. And nothing is left out. Not a single particle of dust is excluded from this beauty, no matter how "unsightly," "scary" or "awkward."

You see it radiating from every object of your affection, and simultaneously, that same beauty radiates from within you, out to the world. No longer believing in the existence of boundaries, separation and division fall away. Free of pride and full of gratitude and authentic humility, you can't help *but* see perfection all around you. In that seeing, you know you *never* had imperfections - you just believed you did because you were taught to believe you did.

Embracing who you are *as* you are, you watch guilt, shame and remorse drop away. And with it, hope and fear, too. Who needs hope for a better tomorrow when it's always right now? Who needs to seek when what you're looking for is doing the looking? Who needs hope when you accept what is, as is? Since fear is born of separation, who invites fear when there is no separation? Who invites fear when it's seen that nothing external *can* cause our experience of fear? The source of our angst and anxiety was our habitual inclination to view the opposites as never coming together, never arising in unison.

We believed they were divorced from each other, like two good people from a bad marriage. Most of our problems came from believing that the opposites can and should be separated from one another. Most of our shame and insecurity came from resisting or running from the "bad" half, the side we deemed "imperfect" and "flawed." Realizing that all opposites are actually aspects of one underlying reality, we see through the illusion of *imperfection and perfection,* and free ourselves from the pairs of opposites. Consequently, we are liberated from the nonsensical challenges involved in the war of opposites.

No longer do we waste energy trying to hide from (or compensate for) what we may still perceive as the "less than ideal" side of our abilities and characteristics. Dropping that heavy burden we carried for so long, we can't help but notice how much lighter our load is. Recognizing that the point was never to pit one side against the other in search of peace, *we unify and harmonize the polarities by discovering the ground that encompasses both.* Resting in this ground that includes both the "positive and negative" aspects, we transcend both. But, we may ask, if we see the moment as it is without any need to alter or fix it - and if we see all of ourselves as we ARE, without any need to hide or compensate for, will we lose our motivation and drive in the name of progress?

What will happen to us if we see our opposites as one? What will happen if we become actually grateful for our so-called imperfections and see them in an entirely new light?

What if we finally recognize, that without our "less than ideal" half, we couldn't experience who we are, let alone experience anything at all? What might happen if we see the conditions of existence as mutually interdependent upon each other, as the quantum physicists have already proven? With any luck, we'll lose our misperception that our happiness depends on accepting our strengths and resisting our weaknesses. When the opposites of all of our characteristics and traits are seen as one - and *already* in harmony - already and always a beautiful melody of comfort and discomfort, pleasure and pain, insecure and secure, then our old battles and enemies become dances and lovers.

When we empty ourselves of all our notions and opinions, we are left with the fullness and completeness of life - all in perfect harmony. Then, and only, then, are we in a position to make friends with ALL of it, not just half of it.

Then, and only, then, are we in a position to just ENJOY THE RIDE.

www.ingramcontent.com/pod-product-compliance
Lightning Source LLC
Chambersburg PA
CBHW070205060426
42445CB00033B/1549

9780615949130